D1272427

PENAL SERVICES FOR OFFENDERS

Penal Services for Offenders:

m6

Comparative Studies of England and Poland 1984/85

Edited by
THELMA WILSON
Department of Paramedical Sciences
North East London Polytechnic

Avebury

Aldershot · Brookfield USA · Hong Kong · Singapore · Sydney

© Thelma Wilson, 1987

Published by
Avebury
Gower Publishing Company Limited,
Gower House,
Croft Road,
Aldershot,
Hants GU11 3HR,
England

Gower Publishing Company,
Old Post Road,
Brookfield,
Vermont 05036,
USA

HV
9960
.G72
E57
1987

British Library Cataloguing in Publication Data
Services for offenders : comparative studies
   of England and Poland 1984/85
   1. Corrections ---- England 2. Corrections
   ---- Poland
   I. Wilson, C. Thelma
   364.6'0942   HV9649.E5

Library of Congress Cataloging-in-Publication Data
Services for offenders.
   Bibliography: p.
   1. Criminal justice, Administration of--England.
2. Criminal justice, Administration of--Poland.
3. Juvenile justice, Administration of--England.
4. Juvenile justice, Administration of--Poland.
I. Wilson, C. Thelma, 1929-   .
HV9960.G72E57   1987   364'.941   86-31862

ISBN 0-566-05420-5

Printed in Great Britain by
Richard Clay Ltd, Bungay.

Contents

Preface

This publication marks an important step in the development of the comparative professional education programme which began about fourteen years ago. The opportunity to learn by comparing oneself with a colleague doing a similar job in another country has become formalised into The Services for Offenders: Comparative Studies Course. Writing has always been central to the course experience because the emphasis is on the personal and professional development of those taking part. This is not the usual academic excuse for a visable product, but based on the knowledge that delivering oneself of words onto paper is a necessary part of the learning process.

The reader can judge how the warmth and emotional impact of Polish people were received by the English course members and recorded in this publication, whilst at the same time the group were absorbing the structure and function of the Polish penal system in general, and the probation service in particular.

Each chapter is written either by an English course member or a member of staff. This comparative method of learning is so intense and complex that only by sharing the writing among us can we hope to convey to the reader what we each felt. Some readers will wish to pursue points in other texts and should find the bibliography useful. I hope that for some we will raise so many issues that a personal experience of such a course will become the only answer. Those of us who have benefitted from several courses recognise the thirst for knowledge and understanding, both of oneself and others, that they raise.

The views expressed in this publication are those of the writers and not necessarily of their employers.

Eight English probation officers worked closely with eleven colleagues from Poland. Brenda Palmer has given full details of how this was achieved in the Conclusion. The group was saddened by the death of George Henderson after Part I of the course, Martin Chance joined the group for Part II and the visit to Poland. Supporting the nineteen named course members were several times as many colleagues in their offices and institutions in England and Poland and we are grateful for the co-operation of all of them. The continued support of the Chief Probation Officers in England and the Ministry of Justice in Poland was appreciated. Our heartfelt thanks are given to Professor Maria Ziemska of the University of Warsaw, who lead the Polish group.

The office work was shared by secretaries in several offices, though it is not an exageration to say that without the dogged work of Ernastine Owen and Pam Botha in the South East Regional Staff Development office of the Probation Service and Ruby Boad of the Department of Paramedical Sciences office at NELP, the course could not have become a reality. I would like to say a special word of thanks to Ernastine and Pam who have supported this comparative programme since its beginning, as Ernastine has now retired and Pam has taken a different post as the result of re-organisation.

While I am unable to name those who worked with us from the many offices in Poland, our gratitude is none the less sincere.

Booklets resulting from previous courses have been published by NELP, for whom Evelyn Tovey worked as a secretary for many years, and by a series of unexpected coincidences Evelyn has also prepared this manuscript for the publishers. I am indebted to Evelyn and her colleagues at URCHIN, David and Margaret Wasdell, for the application of their combined skills and knowledge to this project. Muriel Hammond has again allowed us to have the use of her wide range of professional librarian's skills and has also produced the single bibliography from the individual references given with each chapter.

Following is a list of those who took part in the programme.

Kay Andrews, Kent Probation Service*
Barry Bright, South East London Probation Service*
Jill Carperter, Inner London Probation Service*
Martin Chance, West Sussex Probation Service*
Mervyn Dawkin, Inner London Probation Service
John Harper, South East Region Staff Development Unit (Staff)*
George Henderson, West Sussex Probation Service
Brenda Palmer, South East Region Staff Development Unit (Staff)*
Gordon Read, Devon Probation Service*
Roger Scofield, Essex Probation Service
John Simmonds, University of Sussex (Staff)
Thelma Wilson, North East London Polytechnic (Staff)
Ivan Zobkiw, Humberside Probation Service*

Stefan Bielen, Ministry of Justice, Warsaw**
Jacek Browinski, Ministry of Justice, Warsaw**
Jolanta Hoppensztand, Warsaw University
Jerzy Kudynski, Ministry of Justice, Warsaw**
Janina Majer, Ministry of Justice, Warsaw**
Barbarab Mikolajewska, Warsaw University
Dr. Zbigniew Piechowiak, Ministry of Justice, Warsaw**
Leslaw Pytka, Warsaw University**
Danuta Siedlecka, Ministry of Justice, Warsaw
Dr. Hab Wanda Stojanowska, Ministry of Justice, Warsaw**
Eva Widel, Warsaw University
Maria Ziemska, Warsaw University (Staff)**

*Contributors to this book
**Presented a paper to the course in Warsaw

C. Thelma Wilson (Editor)
September 1986

Introduction

JOHN HARPER

Despite the growing popularity of 'going abroad' members going on exchanges express a range of feelings ranging from excitement and challenge to apprehension and doubts. Unlike a holiday, where individuals make their own plans and arrangements and choose their destination, the exchange is determined by the organisers. The two week period in the foreign country is organised by the hosts and although details are given in advance, specific information is lacking. The anxiety generated by uncertainty acts as a stimulus for everyone to prepare and think more specifically about their expectations. Additionally, there is something special about a visit to an Eastern Block country, like Poland.

On both occasions that similar programmes have been undertaken by groups of probation officers, there have been members with family connections, work or war time experiences in Poland. For them the visit has an added significance, they want to find out more about the country, its history and traditions and to test out their impressions. For others with no personal links, the prospect of the visit evokes a mixture of fantasy and curiosity. They all have second hand information and pictures derived from the media and other sources. As one member wrote, 'It is perhaps natural that as we prepared for our visit we were conscious of a strong feeling of anticipation, accompanied by a considerable amount of speculation'.

Poland has been in the headlines for some time with Solidarity, Lech Walesa, Martial Law, the Pope, financial problems and Polish films on television. The popular stereotype is of a country which is a police state, run by a communist government with a strong army and police force, with bugging and censorship commonplace and little or no freedom of action or speech.

When we met the English group to prepare for the visit these images of going behind the iron curtain prompted considerable anxiety and questions about survival and security:

- Are telephone calls and letters censored?
- Can we phone home?
- Will we be restricted?
- Will we be shadowed by the secret police?
- Why can't we buy Polish currency in England?
- What sort of food do they eat?
- Is there a health service?
- Are we in danger?
- Are we free to talk about everything?
- What about bugging devices?

This sample of questions reflects the powerfulness of the popular images generated by the media about life in a communist state.

At a professional level there were many questions about whether we would be told the 'truth' about what really happens inside prisons and in the penal system, how free would we be to see for ourselves what happens and to ask questions and what restrictions would be imposed. They were also concerned about Polish courts, fearing they would be more like military tribunals. The language barrier raised doubts about whether it would be possible to communicate properly about sensitive and detailed issues. They feared they would only receive the official Party line.

Those with experience of Poland tried to tone down some of the wilder fantasies and fears by providing information, but it was noticeable how this often raised fresh anxieties as they heard about the 'black economy' and street traders soliciting for 'hard' currency.

By the end of the induction day everyone was clearer what they had to prepare if their visit was to be valuable to their professional development. They were encouraged to write down their areas of interest and special concerns, contact their partner, visit the library, talk to previous visitors. How to survive away from the familiar in a foreign unknown country was the dominant message everyone took away with them.

At the airport there was a high level of joking and nervous laughter as members said their farewells to family and friends as though they might never seem then again! Once in the air there was no going back. The mixture of Poles returning home laden with bags brimming with Western consumer goods and Poles living in England visiting their families and friends gave the first real taste of what was in store. The chatter of an incomprehensible language, the regular supply of vodka and beer and the Polish newspapers created a mini Poland in the air.

The processing of incoming visitors at Warsaw airport set the scene for much of what life was to be like for the next 14 days. Lengthy queues formed instantly, there appeared to be no sense of order nor concern for time as everyone waited patiently to collect their luggage and to have their visas and passports checked and stamped, usually by a young looking soldier. Once through this experience everyone felt relieved until they saw the Customs procedure. Returning Poles have all their luggage searched with clothes scattered and personal questions asked. The sight of those in front undergoing this humiliating experience with apparent acceptance of the inevitable, re-awakened many of the earlier fears. But despite all this everyone was successfully processed and reached the welcoming sight of our hosts. At least we were expected and would be looked after.

The airport experience and the coach ride set the scene for the dominant issue to prevail for the two weeks and beyond. Here is a country full of visible paradoxes and contradictions. Extremes of poverty and wealth exist side by side, newness rubs shoulders with antiquity, Catholicism is everywhere evident and this is a socialist, secular state where the Polish United Workers' Party is largely made up of non workers. Such examples illustrate the perplexing inconsistencies which are remarkable perhaps because of their ostentation rather than their simple existence, for paradoxes are often a feature of many societies caught up in the process of profound social, economic and political change.

The group were permanently intrigued by their first hand experiences of these contradictions as they struggled to make some sense of them and fit them into their frameworks and cultural assumptions. But the visit was to see and understand how the Polish society perceived and dealt with those for whom perhaps the paradoxes, inconsistencies and conflicts emerged as deviance and more importantly as delinquency.

How to make sense of all this became a major preoccupation,

concern and curiosity.   Whether travelling on public transport or eating and drinking in restaurants or bars, the disturbing evidence was apparent.   One minute people would be having a serious discussion in formal surroundings and the next standing alongside ordinary people struggling to survive in a food or taxi queue.

Members' experiences varied considerably, which reflects how differently individuals cope with and adapt to change and unfamiliar events.   But everyone went through periods of incomprehension and despair: 'I can't understand why the Catholic church is so popular' or 'Why are there so many economic problems?' or 'Why are there such large inequalities between people?' were examples of reflective queries everyone asked at some time or other.   Some sought salvation in ideological explanations, others evaluated each event on its own merit.

As time passed the members became more inquisitive as they strove to explain or make sense of the apparently inexplicable. They wanted answers to questions, to problems, which our hosts did not recognise: 'Why do you invest so much into the needs of the young and yet appear to punish so harshly adult offenders?' or 'Isn't resocialisation a disguised form of repressive social control?' or 'What about individual liberty?' were examples of this.

It is always much easier to see patterns in other people's societies and systems than in one's own and it took some time and confidence before realising that we were there to see and understand the Polish system through their eyes and frameworks and not simply impose our own cultural biases and preconceptions.   Genuine enquiry and investigation involves suspending one's own judgements and being open and receptive to other people's experiences.

The pressure to fit the new experiences into our familiar frameworks was particularly apparent when visiting the provisions for offenders.   Each person thought they knew what was happening and there were always enough similarities to support this view but they had difficulty in 'hearing' what the Polish system was aiming to achieve.   On one visit to a young offender centre there was general agreement that this was the same as the old type English approved school.   Once this was accepted as the basic perception all the questions were focussed on this and it took some time before people started to listen to what the institution was for and how it had come into being.   Of course there were similarities, but there were also many differences.

Resocialisation is the term used by the Polish authorities to describe the purpose of working with offenders. It is used frequently and imprecisely by all staff and officials. For the English it is difficult to understand in concrete terms and it tends to disturb their own values and professional assumptions. At several points members would ask about 'freedom' and 'individual rights', citing Magna Carta as their bible. They were also concerned about 'democratic' decision making. Such questions are meaningless to the Poles, whose society is based on political collectivism and underpinned by the ideology and structure of the Catholic church. Poland has a strong belief in taking responsibility for its young, particularly those who have failed to fit into the main stream society. In some ways they feel they have failed when young people become 'demoralised' (delinquent). Instead of punishing the delinquents they seek to bring them back and retrain them to be 'good' citizens.

For the English, resocialisation is experienced as paternalistic, repressive and stifling of individuality. But whenever they visited centres or projects they were overwhelmed by the warmth, humanity and commitment of all the staff — another example of an inconsistency.

In the field of probation, the Poles make extensive use of voluntary supervisors and employ only a handful of trained staff. On the face of it this is an attractive and sensible system to the English, something to be copied in England. But when they met and talked with some volunteers, the English expressed serious reservations about the volunteers' lack of professional training and identity. The English had difficulty appreciating the Polish rationale for this approach, namely the strongly held belief that offenders are part of the local community and that their rehabilitation should be carried by responsible representatives of that community since they reflect its values and norms.

Judges are much more actively involved in the day to day managing of supervision and the work of the staff. The English were suspicious of 'professional' interference and undermining of the social and psychological aspects of the work. However when they then met judges, they were surprised at their knowledge, understanding and concern for the clients. At one day centre the judges visit regularly, they know all the young people and even join in some of the activities. Whilst this was seen as valuable and even enviable, the English still had reservations.

Those who visited Polish prisons found the experience difficult to assimilate. On the one hand they found the prisons very similar to those in England and yet they felt different in ways that were hard to specify. They talked about their 'militaristic' style, the repressive atmosphere and the harsh physical conditions and tough regime. Yet the system seemed more purposeful and committed than in England – another contradiction.

Wherever the English visited they were confronted with the discrepancy between concern and purposefulness and the poor economic and physical conditions. They admired the attitudes but found the physical realities hard to swallow.

Informally, most of the English group lived with a partner in his or her home. Clearly the hosts took their role to mean showing as much of their country and culture as was possible in the time available. They wanted their guests to experience Poland and to appreciate its beauty, traditions and concerns. Days were long, combining official work with informal activities. The English were frequently exhausted and organised to the point where they began to feel they were losing their own cultural identity. Many were surprised at the Polish pride in 'showing' off their country and several wondered how they presented their own country to visitors. The contrast between the high material standards of the homes of their hosts and those of the majority of the people caused some to wonder about the way a 'communist' state operates. Why do some people have privileges and higher status? Surely everyone is equal? Why do some people have cars and foreign travel whilst the majority have to queue and struggle for their daily existence? These were all the types of questions the English asked. The notion that all societies have some system of social stratification appeared to get lost in the general stereotype of a 'communist' system.

The English were surprised at their 'ambassadorial' status. The Poles wanted to know about political, economic and social issues in Britain. Thanks to BBC World Service and foreign newspapers they were often better informed than the English on some subjects. Their command of English was impressive and humbling. At the many formal functions the English met senior and distinguished Polish personnel who wanted to hear their views, impressions and suggestions for improving the Polish system of justice and welfare. This was not something many of the English experience in the hierarchical and status conscious system in England.

The dominant experience for both groups in 1979 and 1985 visiting Poland was coping with contradictions. On the one hand it is very obviously a foreign country, the language tells you that all the time, and yet there are many apparent

similarities.   The Polish experiences of World War II have
given them a strong sense of attachment to the English who are
seen   as   their   saviours.   This   historically   important
experience tends to make them lean towards the West for support
and reinforcement of their identity.   It was perhaps this
personal feeling that caused the English to be constantly
disturbed and confounded by their experiences.

The Polish warmth, affection and fund of humour added to make
the experience more than just an official visit to study the
Polish system for dealing with offenders.   The Poles went to
great lengths to enable the English to see Poland through their
eyes and experiences.   At times this clearly threatened the
English sense of identity and caused people to find ways of
breaking out of the official programme to have time to rest and
recollect their thoughts.

The experience was extremely potent in many different ways
and we spent several hours over the subsequent six months
processing and analysing the array of impressions, experiences
and perceptions which the visit had generated.   Tolerating
uncertainty, ambiguity and paradoxes clearly are the prime
skills needed to make sense of a visit to Poland.

1 Young offenders, hopes and fears, a comparison between Poland and England

GORDON READ

Abstract

This paper looks at the decline in numbers of juveniles processed by Polish courts and committed to custody in comparison with the increased use of custody for young offenders in England and Wales. The key feature appears to have been Poland's move to use civil court processes to deal with young people. This has some similarities with arrangements in Scotland. It is suggested that the persistence of more punitive approaches in England and Wales is associated with a lay magistracy which takes a fearful, pessimistic and perhaps class view of young people with its actions designed to prevent them challenging the existing social order. Poland, in contrast, has of necessity a more optimistic view of young people, having looked to them for two centuries as its means of salvation from successive occupations.

* * * * *

Aside from the patent egalitarianism of Polish courts and in spite of recent changes in the penal code much criticised by judges and lawyers which make prison mandatory for many offences committed by adults (Financial Times, 1.11.85), one of the most obvious contrasts between the legal systems of Poland and England and Wales lies in their responses to young offenders. Both countries have legislation which enshrines an ameliorative and rehabilitative approach to young offenders. However, while such an approach appears to be effective in Poland - a reduction of juvenile offenders processed through courts from some 60,000 per year both pre and postwar, to 30,000 by the mid sixties (Mosciskier, 1985) - in table 1.1 note how radical this reduction has been - in England and Wales there appears to have been a reverse trend.

Table 1.1
Extracts from Polish Social Statistics 1984

Juveniles (under 17) sentenced by Courts

	1965	1971	1975	1980
Custody	7,408	7,512	4,526	2,944
Non-Custody	22,322	19,110	22,087	14,220
Total	29,730	26,622	26,613	17,164

The actual youth custody population in England and Wales for both males and females, including those committed to custody for fine default, was 17,900 in 1973, 25,300 in 1977, and a staggering 33,200 in 1983 (Bridger, 1985).

It is not easy to compare national figures with any accuracy because of legal and adminstrative changes in both countries. Key changes in 1978 brought juvenile offenders in Poland under the civil jurisdiction of Family Courts, and a large number of offences had been converted from criminal to administrative categories in both 1966 and 1971. In the absence of detailed figures it is difficult to say for certain whether such changes resemble police cautioning practices in England and Wales.

Mosciskier estimates that 25 per cent of offenders in Poland are juveniles whereas they amount to well over a third of offenders in England and Wales. This discrepancy may well be accounted for by legal and statistical factors but differences do appear more fundamental; the Poles taking an optimistic view of young people, concerned to educate and resocialise them if they go off the rails whereas, in England, adults appear to feel more persecuted by the young. The spread of what could be a delinquent syndrome, a conglomeration of behaviour, speech, appearance and attitudes, a frightening ugliness and hostility which pervades human interaction, a crudity, cruelty and violence, a desire to challenge and humiliate and never, but never, to please (Morgan, 1975).

Why this should be so is not entirely clear although, in the interests of comparison, consideration must be given to the wider context of a country's overall collective action for social welfare and placed in an historical context (Rogers, Doron and Jones, 1975).

It might be thought that Poland has had little cause for optimism, having been partitioned by Prussia, Russia and Austria for a century and a half prior to the Treaty of Versailles in 1919, and suffering extraordinary deprivations in the Second World War. It has, however, had opportunities to rethink its social structures: first of all in 1923 and again – having struggled to recover from the effects of war and occupation – in 1959. England, on the other hand, has moved slowly and in an evolutionary manner through major social and political upheavals associated with both World Wars and at the same time remaining true, if that is an apposite word, to a fundamental conservatism, which has enshrined an 18th century class structure within the administration, fabric and vestments of its justice system; urbane and civilised and well able to conceive of young working class males, generation after generation, in the context of Morgan's "New Barbarism".

Sophie Wojciechowski captures the scene in Poland in the postwar years. The prewar welfare system in Poland had many progressive features, but war changed it completely. Over six million Poles perished and another 600,000 were partially or totally disabled. Six years of exploitation left Poland the most impoverished country in Europe. Its industry was destroyed, agricultural resources decimated, the countryside deforested and transportation destroyed. The capital, Warsaw, was 60 per cent demolished. Many schools, hospitals and other social institutions were mined. Large population transfers in a relatively short time resulted from the shift of Poland's boundaries. Poland, a fairly advanced country before the war, suddenly found itself in the category of under developed countries, in need of rebuilding its entire economy (Wojciechowski 1975).

Nocon identifies 1959 as the year in which detailed definitions of the social duties of the state were established in law and which resulted in the building of a network of social counsellors (Nocon, 1982). By 1979, when Poland's Family Courts were reorganised with a welfare as opposed to justice orientation, there were some 58,000 social counsellors with another 7,000 paid workers to provide co-ordination and help with the increasing complexity of social provision required. Much of this focussed on the neighbourhood and offered multi agency solutions through the provision of income maintenance and links with voluntary organisations like the Polish Red Cross, the Polish Committee for Social Welfare (PKPS) or liaison clerks at factories and other industrial units. Wojciechowski certainly confirms Rogers' contention that social security is a by-product of the shift from agrarian to industrial society (Rogers, Doron and Jones, 1975). Social provision in prewar Poland was left very much to the landed gentry - a pre industrial solution - whereas, in addition to the problems identified above, postwar Poland had to engage with a shift of population from rural to urban centres. In 1946, 68 per cent of Poland's population was engaged in agriculture. By 1972 only 46 per cent of the population was so engaged, a shift which has continued as the housing developments outside Warsaw, Krakow and Katowice testify.

Given the country's intense Catholicism and its capacity for survival in the face of the most extreme oppression, it is small wonder that family care became the ideology upon which Polish socialism is built. The Polish code of family law holds the family responsible for the support of its children and for its adult dependents; even brothers and sisters are mutually responsible for each other. The kind of decision seen in the Krakow Family Court would not surprise the Poles: parents and grandparents of an abscondee putative father ordered to pay upkeep towards his child in affiliation proceedings. If these family duties are coupled with the extensive multi agency volunteer organisations in towns, cities, factories and rural co-operatives, it is possible to perceive a potentially effective preventive structure well able to pay attention to its children's activities which, with an economy system devoted to individualism, the English social system currently lacks.

In spite of recent media alarms it would be a mistake to over dramatise English pessimism about the young. We must not over simplify our problems by classifying urban tensions as crude criminality; nor should we over simplify solutions to multi causal problems which will, of necessity, be complex. What is clear from the Polish approach is that its legal code, especially the Acts of 26th October 1982, provides a multi faceted response which enables judges, both paid and unpaid, to hold all matters within their jurisdiction under review in a partnership with probation officers, social counsellors, and family diagnosticians. The potential here is enormous, as the probation officers working with the Family Courts in Krakow were keen to establish. However, they would be the first to say that although the intentions of the Acts of 1982 are laudable, all workers within the system experience problems created by lack of resources, not least of which are poor salaries and status for themselves and other major carers like teachers and residential workers. The Polish structure, seen in both Krakow and Pulawi, offers a good model of neighbourhood concern with a judge and probation officer working in partnership to cover a district court area population of some 35,000 with a structure more in the nature of the Scottish Children's Hearing system than that of the English Juvenile Court.

Laisser-faire is possibly a misnomer for the missed opportunities of England and Wales which were grasped, post Kilbrandon, in Scotland and followed in Poland in 1978 (Celnik, et al, 1982). The English failure seems more a matter of government pusillanimity in the face of pressure groups; an unwillingness to take on magistrates and probation officers rather than change Juvenile Court structures. Rutherford looks at the increasing tendency of English courts to commit juveniles to custody and argues that real choices are made in the generation of such increases (Rutherford, 1984). He castigates government for the increase in prison building and argues forcibly that prison populations are not the inevitable consequences of earlier factors in the system but primarily the consequences of policy choices and practices. He asserts that governments have a choice whether or not to expand prison places, that they need to recognise they have such a choice, that they could target low levels of prison usage and that they should muster the political will to pursue a reductionist course.

Poland, given a different political sytem, has exercised its will in relation to offending behaviour by removing many offences from the penal code to administrative tribunals and also through the use of amnesties: in 1983 the prison population, still massive by English trends, was reduced by 32,000 to about 80,000. The Poles remain punitive towards adults, but in their approach to juveniles they deliberately design measures to replace custody with sentences directed towards the least restrictive sanctions.

One way to account for these differences is to focus on religious belief. Poland is a largely Roman Catholic country with a socialist superstructure directed towards the care of family and the wider society which invests in its youth as its future protection against oppression. Protestant attitudes in England appear to enshrine an individualism which is less dependent on the family though much commended in the context of enterprise. Such individualism, which informed the philosophy

12

of the 19th century has commercial, colonial, even imperial resonances. It cannot be accidental that the first probation officers in England were dubbed "missioners", intervening in the courts of London and other large cities to save young people from drunken excess, to fit them for the training ships and the colonies.

Milham is particularly acerbic on the subject. The 19th century had been preoccupied with child rescue, the perishing classes were to be cleansed in institutions and what was obviously so good for the upper classes in the rapidly expanding Public Schools was duplicated in the Industrial and Reformatory Schools (Milham, 1981). In the case of delinquents, the function of such institutions was clear - he quotes Admiral Field - "I only want to secure a supply of boys for our ships. The schools are intended to train boys for the Mercantile Marines, to supply a waste of life of 4,000 or 5,000 persons drowned every year".

The Centenary publication, The Camera and Dr. Barnardo (Lloyd & Wagner, 1974) implicitly confirms the transportation to Canada - commencing in the year 1882 - of many thousands of Barnardo's Home charges. More telling, in the context of the earlier West African slave trade, and the kind of scapegoating that Morgan inclines to (Morgan, 1975), is the impact of legislation on a little street rough pictured by Waugh - who founded the original Society for the Prevention of Cruelty to Children - it first names him black and then makes him black (Parsloe, 1978).

Milham suggests that serious offences are generally beyond the grasp of young offenders and that they are easily apprehended because of their visibility, catchability and inexperience. Milham also maintains that social class plays a part in protecting some boys from the consequences of their actions. In Poland that is a function undertaken by the Family Courts.

It remains something of a surprise that such punitive attitudes towards the young survive in England and Wales in spite of periods of legislative optimism in 1908, 1933 and that associated with the construction of the Welfare State in the 1940s. Just as the 1908 Children's Act was linked with other reformist legislation and a review of arrangements for social security, the arrival of the Welfare State in the 1940s coincided with an important Criminal Justice Act. This firmly established probation in England and Wales at the same time banishing corporal punishment, penal servitude and hard labour from the penal code.

The Children and Young Persons Act of 1933 was similarly concerned with the welfare of the child but harped back to a preoccupation with institutions: in proper cases to take steps for removing him (the child) from undesirable surroundings and securing that proper provision is made for his education and training - shades of Dr. Barnardo's "Ever Open Door". It was the death in care of a foster child which led to the establishment in 1948 of the new Local Authority Children's Departments with detailed responsibilities for the care of children. 1963 provided a further change; in retrospect almost the one hopeful provision of the rather conservative Ingleby Report (HMSO, 1960), to prevent and forestall the suffering of children, which laid a duty on the Local Authority to provide services, including cash payments, to prevent children being brought before Juvenile Courts and so into care.

The White Paper, "The Child, The Family and the Young Offender" (HMSO, 1965) offered a more radical solution to the needs of children who were delinquent or deprived - the Polish word is demoralised - which might have seen the end of Juvenile Courts as we know them and the establishment of a Scottish system much more in keeping with solutions espoused by France and Poland. However, magistrates and probation officers in England and Wales joined forces to withstand the attack on Juvenile Courts and by the time of the next white paper in 1968 a much modified proposal for reform appeared. This became the Children and Young Persons Act of 1969, which if fully implemented might still have countered the tendency to commit young people to custody. Its most promising feature, Section 5, that children should only be brought to court if they could not be helped by any other means was never implemented. As a result the police retain the power, despite consultation, to bring young people to court.

The aim of the Children and Young Persons Act 1969 was to bring such matters more under civil jurisdiction but civilisation has been slow in coming compared with the process in Scotland. A further attempt to reverse the trend to custody (an increase from 700 to 1,500 to Borstal between 1969 and 1975 and from 2,000 to 4,000 in Detention Centre over the same period) was made with the Criminal Justice Act 1982. However, the ambiguity of that legislation and the provision of powers for magistrates' courts to order up to a year of youth custody has meant that the tide, although not increasing as much as some had feared, swept inexorably on. Parsloe identifies a similar process in relation to American State Legislatures: a lack of tolerance of the normative nature of delinquency and a tendency, having defined the behaviour, to then label youngsters as deviant (Parsloe, 1978).

The Association of Directors of Social Services wrote despairingly in their paper, Children Still in Trouble (1985), that the Children and Young Persons Act of 1969 has resulted in a system accelerating more and more young people into ever harsher custodial regimes, too many, too early, and numbers increasing out of all proportion to the increase in juvenile offending. What this points to is the lack of a coherent policy like that provided for Scotland by the Kilbrandon Report (HMSO, 1964) or the rethink forced upon Polish society postwar which came to the conclusion that the needs of children have little to do with legal categories but require special measures of education and training; social education as Kilbrandon describes it, to strengthen those natural influences for good and to involve parents in decisions about their children.

The comment by Nocon that parallels in actual service provision far outnumber any discrepancies (Nocon, 1982) between England and Poland would certainly bear out the theory of diffusion of emulation of the western climate of opinion described by Rodgers in most spheres, save that relating to juvenile offending (Rogers, Doron and Jones, 1975). The parallels there lie with Scotland or France (itself influenced by the USA) rather more than with England. In both France and Poland government intervention with youth training and the provision of employment has been a crucial plank for the welfare systems. Voluntarism is also important and Poland's approach compares closely to France where thousands of delegues benevoles work to a corps of delegues permanents, both operating in constructive and preventative modes associated with the development of family diagnostic centres linked to Family Court practice and the interests of judges (Rodgers, Doron and Jones, 1975) (Browinski and Jaworska, 1985).

The European approach, French and Scottish, is a major influenced and strength in the Polish system. The continuing interventive role of the judge, authorised by Articles 6 and 7 of the Acts of 26th October 1982 has parallels in the work of Scottish Hearings. That factor coupled with a less mobilisable press, may account for the Polish willingness to persevere with children. In the Polish system the probation officer, who is the main social counsellor, works in a way much more akin to the social workers employed by the old Children's Departments in England or the social workers now associated with Children's Hearings in Scotland. In this sense the probation officer is a true social aide to a Family Court and its civil duties with respect to young people.

In the Krakow voyvod the Family Court has two senior judges, eight judges, eight probation officers and eighty volunteer probation staff dealing with some 1,600 children under one form or another of supervision.   The Court also has six family diagnostic teams (usually psychologist and psychotherapist) to cope with the large numbers of family, guardianship, care and divorce cases concerning children.   Judges, family diagnosticians and probation staff work very closely together and supportively with the various organisations and institutions to which the court has access (Dodwell et al, 1982).

Coupled with the egalitarian approach to defendants and witnesses in the Polish system, the freedom to speak, enshrined in Article 19 of the Acts of 1982, affirms the civil as opposed to legal/penal processes which hold sway.   This is one of the key differences between the English Juvenile Court and the Polish Family Court systems.   However much the English system is directed by law to attend to the welfare of the child, the adversarial system and the complex rules of evidence though focussed on civil rights, can work against the child's best interests.

A consideration of the main features of the Polish Acts of 26th October 1982 highlights these points in relation to juveniles.   Article 2 indicates that the measures envisaged by the Act are to be undertaken in cases where minors display signs of demoralisation or have committed punishable acts. Article 3 provides that in such cases the chief consideration should be the wellbeing of minors with emphasis on bringing about favourable changes in their personality and behaviour and, when necessary, ensuring the proper discharge by parents, or guardians, of their obligations. This parental responsibility is extended to other adults in the community by Article 4 which directs that any person who discovers circumstances indicating the demoralisation of a minor – specifically breaches of social conduct, commission of an unlawful act, systematic evasion of obligatory school or vocational training attendance, use of alcoholic liquor or other means of intoxication, prostitution, vagabondage, association with criminal groups – has a social duty to try and remedy such behaviour and above all to report it to the minor's parents or guardian, his or her school, a Family Court, the civic militia or other competent agency (Poland, 1982).

These extensive processes are very like the approach of the Scottish Children's Hearings also being explored in forward looking Juvenile Bureaux and Youth Support Teams in some areas of England and Wales (Northampton, 1984) (Exeter, 1979-85).

While Article 5 resembles Section 1 of the Criminal Justice Act 1982 for England and Wales, the provisions under Article 6 offer much wider scope for forms of intervention, including

(Section 2) a number of matters currently associated in England and Wales with diversion from prosecution programmes, for example repairing damage, making an apology, undertaking educational employment, avoiding specific locations.   Article 7 bears specifically on the duties of parents – one major difference with the philosophy of limited parental accountability articulated by the Kilbrandon Report in Scotland – authorising a judge to order parents to improve the educational, welfare or health conditions of a minor, enter into co-operation with the school, workplace or medical establishment, and repair damage caused by a child.   A judge can even notify the workplace or social organisations to which parents belong about these arrangements.   In addition, and this may be to do with the judicial association with the Public Prosecutor system, the judge has power to waive or caution in respect of an offence brought to the notice of the court.

Bielen provides a detailed account of some of these arrangements and the numbers of youngsters allocated to them during 1984 (Bielen, 1985).

Table 1.2
Allocation to Activities

Voluntary Work Corps	1,436
Boarding School	396
Industrial Patronage	1,569
Vocational Camps (including those run by Family Courts centres)	20,440
Parent lectures	960
Case Reviews (Judge, Probation Officer, etc.)	5,597
Family Diagnostic Reports	1,765

Bielen indicates that of the 167,000 minors under the supervision of the Family Court, some 11,000 would be there for offence matters.   Of that 11,000, 84 per cent would go to probation, 4 per cent to special education, 9 per cent to correctional school and 3 per cent to houses of correction.

Both Bielen and Piechowiak indentify the close co-operation between court staff and the various state institutions including attention to eventual pre-release arrangements (Piechowiak, 1985). Piechowiak identifies the powers of request that an institution can make of a local state administration or industry to provide work and training, accommodation and advance payment against work for young people released into their care. In this respect the Justice Department plays a leading role, mobilising a system of aid via the Counci of Aid to Minors which has local panels which include social counsellors, probation officers, judges, teachers, as well as union representatives and industrial executives.

The Girls' Centre at Falenice provides a good example of all that is best in the Polish system. It has many similarities with the better English Children's Homes with Education, like Peper Harow in Surrey. Falenice is a Bail Centre for girls aged 13 to 17, a Detention Centre for those up to 21, and it also offers family diagnostic facilities, a school and training in hairdressing, dressmaking and sewing. It has recreational activities, drama, poetry, painting, as well as opportunities for sport including skiing expeditions. The minimum stay is six months, the maximum lasting up to the age of 21. Girls there are not treated as criminal so much as unfortunate and unhappy, with staff very anxious to help them improve their self-esteem and provide creative solutions to their problems as well as encouraging family contacts. While offences of all kinds have been committed by girls held at the centre, most are for theft or group shoplifting. One creative solution offered to a lesbian girl who had a fear of being confined was to be allowed out to a job in a factory where she could take her place amongst the lads; a successful outcome as it turned out.

At the other extreme are the large houses of correction and youth prisons which may hold up to a thousand youngsters. They are penitentiary in style but focus on work and education with the offer of conditional release in the knowledge of full employment and a range of assistance once released. One of the most striking differences between youth institutions in Poland and England was their industrialisation, the hum of activity and the opportunities for training. Youngsters are released with certificates of qualification which enable them to take up places in factories and other work outlets. The disadvantage, of course, is that sentences are often indeterminate and youngsters can be kept away from their home environments for long periods, which make resettlement difficult. That and the other life as Pytka describes institutionalisation (Pytka, 1985), and the power of the sub-culture means that as in England the rehabilitative effect of institutions has severe limitations. This is in spite of the rather more constructive use of work outlined by Replinzki, men being able to earn a living wage through which to support a family and make reparation (Replinzki, 1981).

It was difficult to discover accurate information about the demography of age groups in Poland, once the population explosion of 1946-60 is discounted. A decline in juvenile offending may indeed be a function of the decline in the number of young people overall. In England and Wales there has been some interesting work on this by Pratt (Pratt, 1985) and Pease (Pease, 1985). This suggests that Poland will need to guard against the English phenomenon of building more institutions to house a higher proportion of fewer offenders. This tendency is in spite of the decline in absolute numbers of offenders which also contrasts starkly with the contraction of school building because of the shortfall of pupils in secondary education predicted up to 1990. Custody received 6 per cent of juvenile disposals in England and Wales in 1971 and 12 per cent in 1981. The paradox identified by both Pease and Pratt concerns studies of population cohorts in 1953, 1958 and 1963 which have two clear features. The first is that 30 per cent of all males in the cohort would be convicted of a standard list offence by the time they were 28, with 70 per cent of those not reoffending after the first offence. The second is that 5 per cent of those males account for something like 70 per cent of all convictions.

Table 1.3
Juvenile Offenders

Year	No. of Indictable Offences (Juveniles)	No. of Cautions (Juveniles)	Totals
1974	93,000	91,600	184,600
1975	91,200	88,200	179,400
1982	86,700	93,600	180,300
1984	70,100	99,000	169,100

Another factor, bearing out Walker's earlier studies, suggested that a second conviction is in any case more likely to follow an interventive disposal like probation (Walker, 1966). As Milham indicates it is the persistent offenders who defy the filters that are the continuing problems of the services which tackle juvenile crime (Milham, 1981), and who, once in the system stay, their reality disintegrating under the bewildering array of experiences. To some extent this trend to custody is even more bizarre insofar as the development of diversion schemes, under the auspices of Juvenile Bureaux, have had a more marked effect since the passing of the 1982 Criminal Justice Act as Table 1.3 indicates (HMSO, 1985).

The building of more institutions in the face of that kind of evidence is nothing if not perverse.

From this account of English and Polish systems there emerge two key themes which are to do with attitudes and structures. Poland is optimistic about young people. It is a country which must have faith in the capacity of its young, generation after generation, to surmount oppression. In England, if account is to be taken of Morgan's pessimism (Morgan, 1975), the reverse seems to be the case with juvenile courts somehow saddled on behalf of society with attitudes associated with the suppression of the young, as if the young are potential revolutionaries.

It is therefore strange to consider how matters are in Scotland, even though, like Poland, their adult courts are harsh towards adults: once separated out from the general prison statistics of the United Kingdom, Scotland has the highest number of prisoners received into prison per 100,000 of population in Western Europe (Fitzmaurice, 1982). Juvenile Courts in Scotland were replaced in 1971 by Children's Hearings staffed by lay people but serviced by a Reporter, an official with experience as a lawyer or social worker. The Hearings have no power to try issues of fact and are concerned only with the resolution of the case before them. Proceedings are based on the consent of the child and his or her parents with the adviser — the Reporter — to the Hearing as the key figure in the system with the function of deciding on the information available whether or not a child may be in need of compulsory measures of care. If a Reporter considers this is the case the child will be referred to the Children's Hearing. If there is no indication that the child needs such measures of care the Reporter may do nothing at all, may arrange voluntary help from the Social Work Department or school, or may interview or write to the child and the parents outlining the possible consequences of the child's actions. The common element in all these measures is that they lack compulsion (Manchester, 1985).

While the dispositions are nothing like as extensive as those contained in the Acts of 26th October 1982 for Poland, they can nonetheless be relatively comprehensive because of the conditions which can be attached to the arrangement under which a child may be placed under the supervision of a social worker. Supervision may be with or without conditions but can include residence in the equivalent of a Community Home with Education. If this is the case the Hearing must specify the location. While no time limit is placed on such an order, it may be reviewed on request and must be reviewed annually by the Hearing. Interestingly, there is no power to fine or commit to a Detention Centre or Youth Custody Centre, although children may still be dealt with in the court system for serious offences – murder or rape, or offences where the child is charged with an adult.

One feature of the operation of the Scottish system which contrasts with England and Wales is that the recruitment to the Hearing panels is broadly amongst the age group 30-40 with limits of five and at the most ten years of participation (Manchester, 1985). By contrast, the English magistrate may sit on the Juvenile Court Bench until the age of 65.

One hope for the English system may be the influence of conciliation as it is applied in civil hearings in relation to divorce and custody issues: making the court into much more of a Hearing so that people can put their point of view without being interrupted on matters like the rules of evidence. On the wider front, in the United States and in England, there is a debate about prevention which the Poles appear to take very much for granted: that is, whether to intervene with school organisations, family and neighbourhoods, or whether the focus should be on individual change. The dualistic fallacy that some are delinquent and some not by virtue of official reactions to delinquent acts has been criticised by Johnson (Johnson, 1981) who is also sceptical about preventive work in schools. It is Farringdon (Farringdon, 1985), an English criminologist with an interest in cohort studies, who expresses some optimism about preventive approaches. He examines the Perry pre-school project which has a resemblance to a day nursery programme for young children supervised by the family section of the Krakow court. The Perry project (Schwinhart and Weikart,1980) was for lower IQ, lower class black children in a 'Head Start' programme and the results suggest that pre-school enrichment can lead to increased school success and ultimately to decreased delinquency.

Such success seems to result from a much closer involvement with young people in their neighbourhood setting with directed both to the home environment and also to improving the youngster's problem solving skills and social competence generally. The glimmerings of this preventive approach may be seen in the British Government's extended education and training programme associated with the Youth Training Schemes and Community Programmes themselves brought about by chronic unemployment difficulties amongst the young: 25 per cent of males aged between 17 and 19 failed to obtain jobs in 1985. In Poland, whatever the state of the national debt, full employment has to date been a feature of the nation's stability. Employment skills are recognised in all state institutions as essential for successful rehabilitation and it is clear that employment in England is one of the main aids to a successful transition from adolescence to adulthood. Without it there will be much social and psychological damage aside from the fact that being unemployed tends to make courts, and Juvenile Courts amongst them, more punitive.

If England can learn anything from Poland it is to recognise that real solutions lie not in intensive alternatives to please magistrates but in structures more sympathetic to the problems of the young with offence resolution rather than punishment and with the kind of educational focus enshrined in Polish law.

"Diversion" approaches developed by the Juvenile Bureau in Northampton and the Exeter Youth Support Team point the way ahead. They give much attention to no further action warnings sanctioned in the advice given to Chief Constables by Home Office Circular 14/1985, which is very similar to arrangements outlined in Articles 2 to 5 of Poland's Acts of the 26th October 1982.

Short of a radical change of England's Juvenile Courts and the traditional approaches of probation and social work staff associated with them, the initiatives of the Juvenile Bureaux, which involve police, social workers, probation officers and education workers in enterprises of co-operation may be in our children's best interests for the future by diverting them from process, prosecution and from custody in all its guises.

What Poland appears to offer its young is humanity. They are treated as if they are the children of a family. Jerome Miller, quoted by Rutherford (Miller, 1985) and wellknown as a man who closed the Massachusets juvenile institutions, urges that sentencers should not do anything to a child or young person that they would not willing permit done to their own children. A pragmatic and feeling touchstone such advice echoes Francis Hobler, magistrate, giving evidence to the Select Committee on the State of the Police in the Metropolis of London, in 1815 (Parsloe, 1978): For as men and as parents they must feel for the situation of such characters (children in Newgate Prison).

2 An examination of the forces that influence criminal justice policy and its administration in England and Poland

BARRY BRIGHT

Abstract

In a pluralistic, social democratic country such as England, inconsistent and ambiguous ideologies are reflected in criminal justice policy and its administration.

In a centralist, socialist country such as Poland, a consistent, clear ideology is reflected in criminal justice and its administration.

This paper will attempt to analyse these hypotheses. It will be helpful to have in mind two conceptual models of society: the order model and the conflict model which will be referred to as the issues are examined.

* * * * *

To satisfy the test of pluralism, a society must rest on a value consensus, with power scattered among balanced and diverse interests, and the state as a value-free framework to moderate and contain struggles. To satisfy the test of social democracy, a society must have free elections, freedom under the law, freedom of speech, freedom of assembly, the right to

23

protest and strike, an unfettered press and media.

A number of factors determine criminal justice policy in England and Wales. Clearly of fundamental importance is the role played by central government because of the power it wields. This power is affected by the will and confidence of its leaders, the state of the opposition and the nature of the policies themselves. It is also influenced by the extent of its electoral strength and general government policy.

The role of parliament is somewhat limited because of the nature of the political system with power being vested in the executive. Parliament is primarily an arena for discussion of government policy and as such has an important communication function. At times of a small parliamentary majority the situation is different. More detailed examination of government bills occurs at the Committee Stage, and All-Party Penal Committees act as watchdogs. These committees are advised by interested bodies: both professional associations (National Association of Probation Officers [NAPO], Prison Officers Association [POA]) and pressure groups (National Assocation for the Care and Rehabilitation of Offenders, National Council for Civil Liberties). Vested interest groups are strong in mitigating the force of legislation – some are more powerful than others and influence legislators in a variety of ways.

The Home Office plays an important role because of its power and position and its continuity. Its thinking is influenced by outside advisers, both pressure groups and academics. The very position of such a major organ of state as the Home Office lends itself to conservatism, and because of the sensitive issues with which it has to deal, there is a tendency for it to develop a defensive stance and at times a siege attitude.

Criminologists have also played a part in influencing policy. Their preoccupation with the criminal and the impact of custody have focussed thinking on the individual and punishment. However, in recent years even this has changed with the introduction of a wider perspective concerned with societal and structural factors.

There has generally been a shared attitude by the rank and file members of the political parts and their adoption of a pre-punishment stance which has curbed the more rehabilitative tendencies of liberal but rather weak Home Secretaries. Practitioners in the criminal justice field – the police, the judiciary and magistracy, prison staff, probation (operating as they do from different ideological bases) all wield varying degrees of influence on policy and more especially on its administration.

Another major factor is that of public opinion and how it is formed, presented, stimulated and used. This focusses attention on mass media and advertising – subjects which will be referred to subsequently. A particularly potent factor is that of the dramatic crisis or horrendous crime which prompts outraged public opinion to demand rapid action. The major social and economic conditions of the day, e.g. unemployment and the tensions and rifts they cause in society, also affect criminal justice policy.

It would be surprising if the complex interplay of all these elements and the underlying ideologies did not produce ambivalent and confused criminal justice policies and practices. What occurs depends on the relative strengths and alliances of the forces involved. One example will service to illustrate. The 'care' ideology of the Children and Young Persons Act 1969 was central to the paper 'Crime – A Challenge To Us All' prepared for the Labour Party in 1964. This led to the White Paper 'The Child, the Family and the Young Offender' in 1965, and after deliberation to a further White Paper 'Children in Trouble' in 1968. The idea of Family Courts was dropped and an 'offence clause' added to the list of conditions which warranted, together with the 'need' condition, the making of an Order. The 1970 election brought a change of government with a different orientation. It did not repeal the Act but did not implement the 'offence' condition as a test for a Care or Supervision Order which remained in itself a reason for court proceedings (albeit after reference to the Juvenile Bureau). This shows the outcome of the struggle between the proponents of the 'welfare' and 'justice' models.

The subsequent reorganisaton in England and Wales of local authority Social Services Departments and the different orientations of the new generic social workers led to a certain crisis of confidence in the Juvenile Courts which eventually led to the introduction of the Residential Care Order. The laudable and far-sighted objectives of the Act have been contradicted in practice and the Act failed to overcome the neglect and apathy which pervaded the whole field of juvenile crime for many years (Berlins, 1974).

Major economic and social changes have taken place in England in recent years. The Conservative government's monetarist policies and attempts to make British industry more competitive have wrought a high social cost in terms of large scale unemployment and increasing poverty. Ideological emphasis on the individual and personal freedom has led to cuts in welfare and social services provision. In 1972 the word 'mugging' was introduced into the criminal justice vocabulary and with it a whole set of connotations and feelings. This has led to the notion of 'moral panic'. This is a situation in which societal reaction to a perceived series of events clearly outweighs their actual threat (Ryan, 1983).

Frequent and particular presentation of dreadful crimes helps to create an impression that England is in an increasing state of lawlessness and feeds on the legitimate fears of the vast majority of ordinary people who have no direct contact with crime. Insufficient professional and public attention has been given to the British Crime Survey (Home Office 1983), the findings of which contrast starkly with the sensational pictures of crime in the popular press (NAPO, 1985). It also found that people are less punitive towards lawbreakers than usually imagined, which runs counter to the conventional wisdom that public opinion demands tough sentences.

New criminal justice policies and their administration throw light on the relative power of those involved. The Criminal Justice Act 1982 sounded the death-knell of the 'rehabilitative ideal' and heralded the 'justice principle' in young adult institutions, by ending indeterminancy. It also spelled out that custody should only be used as a last resort but this has not happened in practice, which shows the power of sentencers and perhaps the ambivalence and lack of initiative of probation officers. An amendment to the Act overturned an earlier House of Lords ruling with regard to the status of day centre conditions in Probation Orders. The 1982 Act also introduced the restrictive Night Restriction Order which through the combined efforts of the Probation Service and Justice clerks has been largely unused by sentencers.

In 1982 the Home Office embarked upon a review of the Probation Service and subsequently produced its Statement of National Objectives and Priorities, the theme of which was that services have to be fitted into available resources thus providing a 'management by objectives' thrust to the administration of the Service. What will happen in practice is subject to local plans.

In October 1983 the Home Secretary announced a major expansion of the prison building programme - an extra 10,600 places by 1991. A decision warmly supported by the POA and opposed by NAPO.

It is relevant to comment on the changing ideologies in the Probation Service in England and Wales. For many years the service espoused the 'medical model' with its emphasis on the knowledgeable expert 'treating' the 'sick' client.

Reservations by practitioners and the writings of academics (e.g. Bottoms & McWilliams, 1979) have changed professional thinking. However the changes have been patchy and have led to some confusion and a weakening of the collective voice of the service both in practice and in influencing policy.

Turning to Poland, it is perhaps wise to say that it is not easy to write briefly about this complex country because of the twists and turns in its history, the character of its people, and the contradictions in Polish life. Its geography, large, flat and without natural frontiers, has made it prey to a whole series of invaders from all sides over the centuries which has left a particular legacy in the national consciousness - that of survival (whatever the odds). It was partitioned three times in the late eighteenth century and from 1795 - 1918 did not exist as an independent state. The new state then survived for twenty years before being subjected to the merciless tyranny of Nazi occupation, which in turn was succeeded by a further form of tyranny under Stalin, especially in the period 1949 - 1954.

The nature of the Polish political system was described by the East German dissident Rudolf Bahro as a 'politbureaucratic dictatorship' (Ash, 1985). Supreme power is vested in the Party's politbureau with the regime's character being moulded by the personality of the leader. Policy is transmitted to society by the Party and State administration.

The security of the regime depends at all times on the potential coercive power of the security and armed forces. The structure is totalitarian and monolithic but day to day politics are fraught with tensions and contradictions (Ash, 1985).

There is a heavy bureaucratic structure in which loyalty is rewarded through promotion. This leads to lack of enterprise, inefficiency, and scope for those who know how to play the system.

Polish communism, unlike that in other Eastern European countries, is distinguished by 'half measure' in that it failed to collectivise agriculture and failed to subjugate the church. These two bastions of pluralism have been preserved (Ash, 1985).

This theme of 'half measure' has been a constant thread in recent Polish history. During the late 1970s , with loans from the West, consumerism and rising expectations increased. However, the economy based on heavy industry meeting political rather than economic goals, moved progressively towards crisis.

This led to shortages and a growing sense of anger and disillusion, so that some turned towards drink and others towards drugs. The black market flourished and there was general resentment of inequality and widespread corruption. There was a covergence of opposition (workers, intellectuals, church) somehow cemented by the visit of a Polish Pope. The conditions for revolution were ripe. What happened is now a piece of major European and world history - not only was Solidarity a free Trades Union, it was also a great social movement, encompassing all aspects of society and a revolution of the soul (Ash, 1985).

Solidarity in the form it then took was crushed in December 1981 by the organised force of the state machine. The very factor which led to its spread of power - telecommunications - led to its downfall with the cutting of the lines. It has always stood for peaceful change and faced with the choice of widespread chaos and death or capitulation, it chose the latter. Since then the government has attempted to 'normalise' society, i.e. bring it back into a state of abnormality. In the Eastern Bloc this process has two stages: firstly direct methods so that subjects are unable to oppose; secondly indirect methods, e.g. raising the standard of living, so that subjects are unwilling to oppose. Here again the 'half-hearted' nature of government action influenced by the power of the church and the hold of Solidarity in the national consciousness meant that the first stage was never fully completed, unlike Hungary and Czechoslovakia.

This brief recent history of Poland is given as a dramatic backcloth to criminal justice policy in Poland. It is not easy to make particular connections but to ignore such events would in itself distort the picture.

Polish penal policy as measured by the high percentage of the adult population serving prison sentences, is one of the most repressive and punitive in Europe, and it is associated with societal attitudes favouring institutionalised ways of dealing with delinquents (Kolankiewicz, 1985). In 1983 the prison population was 83,000 out of a population of 37 million; in 1980 it had been 105,000 and in 1970 71,000 (Mosciskiev, 1985). The crime figures themselves have decreased but this is due to the transfer of certain offences to the category of transgression and dealing with them by special committee but with powers of incarceration of up to three months.

The underlying principle of Polish criminal justice policy with adults is based on punishment and protection of the public; with minors, under eighteen, it is based on re-education. The new law of October 1982 with regard to minors distinctly suppresses the clear penal attitude characteristic of former provision, also the law has been based on the principle that the primary educational duty lies with the parent.

The foreword to the Act of October 1982 states the preparation of the drafts had been preceded by long discussion among professionals – scientists and lawyers – as well as among representatives of a wide range of public opinion. It would be interesting to know more about this and the relative strengths of those involved, especially in relation to the power of the state.

The law introduced new flexible measures for counteracting demoralisation and delinquency. Measures which are based on resocialisation in institutions and followed by reintegration into society.

The importance of the family is fundamental in Polish society and this is supported by tradition, the state and the church. The family is the primary socialising agent and its function needs to be supported and augmented. Parents are well aware of their responsibilities. Should measures to support the family fail, the state assumes responsibility for ensuring the re-socialisation of the demoralised minor.

To see this issue in numerical perspective, those measures which leave the delinquent in freedom constitute 84 per cent. Of the 16 per cent who receive institutional care, 7 per cent are placed in Correctional Schools and 7 per cent in Houses of Correction (Bielin, 1985). The former are similar to Children's Homes and the latter are special resocialisation institutions.

Whilst recognising that there are different practices in the Houses of Correction depending on style, personality and confidence of the Director and the staff, there is a consistent ideological theme, organisation and agreed practice. There is a shared belief by academics, policy makers and practitioners, in resocialisation, which for those who are seriously 'demoralised' takes time to effect, and requires a closed environment with a behaviour modification regime. There is a strong emphasis on education, trade training, co-operative values, and preparation for life outside. The system is based on rewards and punishments, regular assessments and gradual easing back into the community, still under the auspices of the institution.

Careful attention is paid to after care and help with lodgings (which are difficult to find), and work (which is easy

to find), as well as material aid. Finance is provided by a 5
per cent deduction out of inmates' remittance from work, in all
institutions (Piechowiak, 1985). A Council of Aid to Minors
exists under the Ministry of Justice and involves
representatives from the Ministries of Health, Social Welfare
and Education, and local agencies. There is a strong sense of
coherence and confidence in the resocialisation process by
policy makers and practitioners, although a cautionary note was
sounded by one academic stating that in correctional
institutions in many cases the over stringent supervision of
youth occasions frustration and causes anti-social inmate sub-
cultures (Pytlea, 1985). He also refers to difficult staff
relations with each other and with the Director. The belief
in the rehabilitative model, locating the problem in the
individual and/or the family, is one on which it is easier to
develop a policy. It is similar to that which was in vogue in
England a generation ago. Is England ahead or behind? Is
the model too myopic by failing to recognise societal forces,
for political as well as therapeutic reasons, or has England
diversified its thinking because it never created the
conditions fully to test the model's efficiency?

In the Polish criminal justice system key roles are performed
by pedagogues (social educators) and psychologists where
adolescent and young adult offenders (aged 17 - 25) are
concerned. Their strength derives from their own knowledge
corpus and professional identity. Probation Officers,
relatively new practitioners in the field and doing a variety
of jobs such as supervising offenders and volunteers, writing
different reports, have a less significant, although growing,
part to play. They are small in number and work to Judges,
from whence comes their authority. They are not social
workers and have no firm professional base. Their income and
conditions of service are poor - they do not have secretaries
and few have cars - a nightmare in rural areas. They do not
belong to an independent organisation, have no professional
association and rarely meet together. On the optimistic side
there are signs that their status and incomes may increase -
albeit to a limited extent.

It is interesting to compare their position with Probation
Officers in England, where by tradition officers have an
important measure of professional autonomy, have a competent
professional association and Trade Union, operate from a social
work value base, have good working conditions and operate in a
reasonably supportive management structure. They have
considerable opportunity to influence practice and some
opportunity to influence policy, e.g. the National Association
of Probation Officers (NAPO), a persistent voice against
preparing reports in 'not guilty' Crown Court cases seems at

last to have been recognised in the recent Home Office draft circular. NAPO has also played an important campaigning role in the policies of payments of Department of Health & Social Security benefits to homeless clients. NAPO also has links with other interest groups e.g. Campaign for Homeless and Rootless (CHAR).

To change focus: alcohol has been a growing social problem in both countries. Such was the concern in Poland that new legislation was introduced in October 1982. The preface to the provisions stated that in recognition of the fact that a life in sobriety is essential to the moral and material well-being of the Nation, it has been enacted. It is significant that the problem is perceived as being against the state's interest. The thrust of the legislation was to reduce the use of alcohol, change the structure of consumption, initiate and support schemes for changing the habits in the use of such beverages, to further temperance in workplaces, to prevent and remove the consequences of alcohol abuse and to support the endeavours in these fields of social organisations and workplaces. This required a range of measures: social control, education, health and penal. The importance of the exercise and the centralist power and its organisation is seen in the structure set up to deal with the problem. A Council of Ministers will form a Commission for the Control of Alcoholism to act in an advisory role. Local agencies will appoint similar commissions for the control of alcoholism and will co-ordinate activities of all local health, education cultural agencies.

Three per cent of annual value sales of alcohol was to be allocated out of state budget to fund detoxification and treatment centres. Alcohol was forbidden to be sold at work, in places of mass assembly, on public transport, in catering establishments between 6 a.m. and 1 p.m., and at sports grounds. The alcohol content in drink was to be reduced.

The Act established a range of voluntary treatment agencies and social control measures where those causing family problems, work or social problems through drink could go for treatment, if necessary under supervision of a probation officer. For those who sell drink illegally the maximum punishment is two years' imprisonment. This is a comprehensive set of measures, involving education, voluntary and compulsory treatment and punishment.

It is difficult to know how effective these steps have been. Many turned to distilling their own drink and there are still alcoholics on the streets of Warsaw. According to one account although alcoholism, which affected four and a half million adults, is seen as a social evil, the intensity of the condemnation is weak. Unfortunately this point is not amplified.

In England over 1000 will die at Christmastime in road accidents, many caused by drink. There are a variety of measures for trying to cope with this problem but they lack widespread organisation and are up against formidable sectional interests, not the least the government which relies heavily on alcohol taxation and the strong drink lobby, with persuasive advertising, and ambivalent public opinion. The issue is far from simple and involves complex issues of freedom and the political organisation of society.

The drugs problem is a major concern in both countries. In both countries it is a problem of alienated, disaffected youth, it involves 'hard' drugs and has serious criminal elements. The major difference is that in England drugs are imported, while in Poland there is a ready access to domestic heroin as poppies are widespread and poppycake is a traditional dish.

In both countries medical and therapeutic community models are used. In England the state's main funding is to medicine and the voluntary sector's to therapeutic communities. In Poland medical treatment has fallen out of power due to its ineffectiveness and the main hope lies in the development, albeit small at present, of resocialisation centres called Monar. The first experimental centre was established in 1981 and proved to be sufficiently efficacious for the system to be developed (Kolankiewicz, 1985).

The underlying principle is that of resocialisation through institutional experience – in this case a particular kind of open, responsibility-giving, anti-failure culture with an emphasis on group support, work on the land, education and gradual re-introduction into society, with subsequent back up from the institution. The message is that in order to change the addict needs motivation, support, time and a whole new therapeutic environment promoting emotional health and social responsibility, re-inforced by a changed social environment, friends, centred on return to the community.

Similar, and different, therapeutic communities operate in England and there has recently been a big publicity push to help drug abusers as well as extend government powers to reduce trafficking and punish the prime movers both through inprisonment and confiscation of their assets. There is still some distortion in public opinion with street dealers seen as 'Mr. Big' rather than as desperate fellow-abusers.

Work is important in Polish life. The structure of society is such that there is no unemployment, though gross under-employment there may be. It is the duty of the individual to work. To back this up the Act of October 1982 introduced measures concerning procedure in relation to persons evading employment. The law spells out that male Polish nationals between 18 and 45 who have not worked for three months and not registered at an employment bureau are required to explain why they are not in work and how they are managing to cope financially. They can be directed to work and if they persistently evade work their names will be placed on 'the list'. Criminal action will be taken in the case of misdemeanours, e.g. tax evasion. Failure to do community work can result in a fine or three months' custody.

Work plays a significant part in the resocialisation process both in terms of trade and skills training, working out from institutions and general preparation for work on release. There is an important measure of coherence here with the meeting of both individual and society needs.

In England debate rages over the links between unemployment and crime. Although statistical evidence cannot be produced to link them, it can be demonstrated that custodial sentences are more likely to be given to defendants who are unemployed. Discussion as to how best to help unemployed probation clients raises ethical as well as social work and practical issues. Trade training continues in Youth Custody institutions but there is little expectation that this will lead to a job on release. Politicians, academics, practitioners have diverse views on the Youth Training Scheme and similar schemes.

In May 1984 the Home Office produced Criminal Justice - a Working Paper and spelled out three underlying themes: (a) the maintenance and encouragement of public confidence in the criminal justice system, (b) the search for greater efficiency and effectiveness, (c) the retention of a proper balance between the rights of the citizen and the needs of the community as a whole. The paper listed a number of issues: public confidence, crime prevention, police powers and effectiveness, court procedures, diversion from custody, the Probation Service, prison population, and the prison building programme, the efficient running of the prison service, victims, and changes in the criminal law.

Each of these issues is open to influence to a greater or lesser extent depending on the power and degree of influence of the interested groups - the police, probation service, prison service. However, a government with a large majority, a strong right-wing orientation, espousing an aggressive social control ideology is likely to be the main determining factor especially as it is operating in a law and order, anti—welfare climate.   Yet, in addition to the continuing power of the ballot box, there are other forces at work — that is over and above concerned liberals and left—wing activists.

The Archbishop of Canterbury's Commission on Urban Priority Areas, 'Faith in the City', has recently been published. Symbolic of its potential effect was the fact that a government spokesman referred to its authors as Marxists and tried to discredit it.   The report describes the most impoverished inner city neighbourhoods and council estates where people are paying — in rising unemployment, decaying houses, falling incomes and the collapse of decent neighbourliness — the price exacted by the new Right for the enrichment of sleeker people and leafier suburbs.   This assessment of the report is by David Donnison, Professor of Town and Regional Planning at Glasgow University, who also refers to 'The British Housing Enquiry' under the chairmanship of the Duke of Edinburgh, in October 1985, and to the Consumer Council's review of social security in August 1985.

1984 saw a major crisis in the fabric of British society with the miners' strike, which raised many complex issues about he nature of English society, government, law, etc.   Inner city riots of 1981 and again in 1985 raise another, similar set of complex questions.   In both these situations the police were at the forefront.   The increasing social polarisation due to government policy certainly makes the project of restoring police legitimacy an uphill struggle (Reiner, 1985).   The police face a difficult task in a divided country and in certain areas the position at times is untenable.   The government's reaction is to 'criminalise' the process and then pursue 'criminal justice' goals.   It is easier and quicker to do this in the present climate than to acknowledge the need to do something to ameliorate the underlying causes.   It is possible to do both.   The Police and Criminal Evidence Act 1984, shortly to take effect, increases police powers in the complex situation of interface with the public.

However, there are new safeguards for suspects.   It is hoped that both will be monitored fairly.   As well as demonstrating the government's intentions the new Public Order Bill also shows the influence at work on criminal justice policy.   Nick Davies writing in The Observer of 8 December 1985 states 'Senior Home Office officials have privately warned that the controversial new offence of disorderly conduct in the Public Order Bill is undesirable and possibly unacceptable to public opinion.   Their warnings were overruled by a concerted campaign by police groups ... Chief Superintendent Ron West,

Secretary of the Police Superintendents' Association said: Initially the Home Office did resist us. They were concerned about public reaction. We acted in concert with the Police Federation and the Chief Officers and the Home Secretary seems to have come down fairly heavily on our side.' A loose coalition of trade unions, pressure groups and minority rights supporters joined the NCCL in a nationwide campaign against the Bill.

As for the Bill itself it seriously underminds the traditional right to protest peacefully and exposes police to accusations of political interference. The Bill should include a positive right to demonstrate. The Guardian leader of 7 December 1985 states that it moves Britain several notches nearer to a society in which any group of people who wish to band together publicly to express a dissident point of view can only do so by grace and favour of the authorities in this case the police force. Political public protest in Poland is dealt with severely.

How can the political and social structure of Poland best be described at present? There is no simple answer. According to George Schopflin, Lecturer in Politics at the London School of Economics and Political Science and the School of Slavonic and Eastern European Studies, a fifth is deeply committed to Solidarity, a fifth to the regime, and three fifths neutral or passively tolerant (Schopflin, 1985).

Solidarity, whose main supporters are drawn from the intelligensia and from amongst skilled workers, operates both over and underground, and is primarily concerned with keeping the spirit of the movement alive in the national consciousness, by publishing magazines, pamphlets etc. in the underground ress, and taking considerable risks in distributing them. Lech Walesa is kept under close official surveillance but continues to shine like a lighthouse. Many sympathisers use particular occasions, safely, to demonstrate their 'Solidarity', e.g. 15,000 attended the funeral of a 19 year old youth who died in police custody. This would support the contention that many live a double life: wary and silent in public, defiant and emotional in the sanctity of the church.

Col. Jaruzelski heads the state machine and its supporters owe their positions to the various institutions and bureaucracies of the state. The elite that now rules Poland is an informal alliance of military politicians and the heavy industry lobby (Schopflin, 1985). The latter continues to run the major heavy industries, coal, steel, heavy engineering, along traditional lines - pursuing political rather than economic ends, a situation that helped create the economic crisis in the Gierek years - the late 1970s. Another grouping is the Communist Party, still resentful at their loss of power and seeking opportunities to retain it, especially as they see themselves and not 'the military' as the rightful leaders of a socialist state.

The role of the church is crucial in Polish society. Traditionally powerful it has become a major beneficiary of the events of recent years. It is seen by the state as having a major stabilising influence, whilst it has picked up the torch of freedom so dramatically wrested from Solidarity's grasp in December 1981. Father Malkowski, a priest in the mould of the martyred Father Popieluszko, states that the church has become the Noak's Ark in a Communist deluge. The Polish Pope continues to have a powerful effect. The church also protects the Arts, whose activities were seriously curtailed when martial law was imposed. According to a well known playwright when that happened something was broken in Poland.

Economically the country is dependent on the Soviet Union for oil, cotton, iron ore, etc. as well as for employment, principally shipbuilding. There have been three economic crises in the past 15 years with serious social consequences. Will there be a fourth? Certainly life is hard for the ordinary Pole: queues and shortages are common, as are lengthy waits for cars, about 10 years, and a flat, about 15 years. Petrol is rationed and money is getting tighter. Timothy Ash concludes his masterful book as follows, the Poles are a free people in an unfree country. A people without Solidarity, but not without solidarity. And persevering in hope (Ash, 1985). My own metaphor for the Poles is that of a scolded, sullen, defiant child, resentful, patient and waiting...

Examination of the political forces, the state of the nation and criminal justice policy in England raises questions as to whether it can confidently be asserted that we live in a social democratic pluralistic society based on an order model. The description 'democratic' still holds true because of the ballot box, although some would argue that local democracy has received a severe blow. Mick Ryan, Senior Lecturer in Humanities at Thames Polytechnic, argues that we live in an authoritarian consensus and a law and order society (Ryan, 1983). The argument is that a right wing, anti-welfare government, together with widespread unemployment, deprivation and poverty, have brought about demoralisation for many and acts of aggression, mindless in nature, by certain groups. This raises the question as to whether we are moving towards a position where the model of society can best be described as 'conflict' - and not just by Marxists.

Many would maintain that there has been a coercive tilt to the criminal justice system as evidenced by the expanding prison building programme, planned and actually restrictive legislation, including new powers for the police, and no change towards a more restitutive system of law for the majority of offenders - like that which pertains for large corporations and tax avoiders.   Should this trend continue apace, with conditions seriously worsening for large deprived groups, then difficult 'political' questions will be raised for the probation service.

In Poland it is not easy to relate criminal justice policy to the complex political structure.   A structure which in some senses could be termed pluralistic and where the term 'socialist' could be questioned.   The coercive forces of the state together with the strength and allegiances of the other significant groups leads one to use the conflict model in describing the country.

Little positive can be said for the Polish penal system for adults, for it is punitive and restrictive.   However, there are definite positives in the system for 'minors'.   The ideology is based on support for the family, and where the family support is not enough, there is a comprehensive, cohesive, integrated system for resocialising the young person. Having said this, one is only too aware of a lack of knowledge as to what actually happens in the institutions, in the minds of those who are being resocialised and in disaffected Polish youth generally.   However there are clues.   At a more observable level the massive turning away from the state and party by Poland's post-Solidarity youth has been symbolised by the spawning of a whole kaleidoscope of sub-cultures.   Some ape their Western counterparts, others take on specific Polish attributes, highlighting a sense of collective malaise. Studied indifference to the authorities' exhortations, an extreme form of live and let live, staying loose, super tolerance, exaggerated democracy are just some of the regalia of the new youth cultures (Kolankiewicz, 1985).

Although there are serious questions about one's original hypotheses about England and Wales it probably just holds true, probably ....   As far as one can tell the complex forces in Polish society have not influenced central control of criminal justice policy, and the policy - for good or ill - does have a consistent ideology.

3 Ideology and crime in relation to juvenile justice systems in England and Poland

KAY ANDREWS

Abstract

The paper considers the escalating trend towards a more punitive attitude towards young offenders in England, and compares this to the situation in Poland. Whilst adult offending is not dealt with in any detail, it is important to note that Poland has distinguished very clearly between young and adult offenders, with the latter being dealt with relatively severely. In contrast England has moved further away from distinctions between the two groups, with an increasing tendency to sentence young offenders to custodial institutions.

In both societies historical, cultural, religious and political differences all appear to have played a part in this process. Polish opinion, the role of the media and the relationship between judiciary and state, have had varying degrees of influence on sentencing policy in both countries. In spite of the seeming differences in attitude towards young offenders, both England and Poland have a high proportion of young people in institutions of various kinds. Whilst Poland may have a more liberal family and child centred approach towards delinquency, and perhaps young people in general, it may still have something to learn about the dangers of 'net widening', inherent in the welfare approach. The paper concludes that both societies appear to rely more on beliefs and ideologies, shaped by national and cultural factors, rather than on a rigorous and analytical examination of deviance and the effectiveness of different responses.

* * * * *

The general attitude of any society towards deviance and offending seems to play an important role in developing the structure of its criminal justice system and services for offenders. Attitudes towards sentencing of offenders may be accommodated within a predominantly 'justice' or 'welfare' based framework of intervention. These frameworks, in turn, may be determined by what is perceived as 'public opinion', which is formulated and expressed in different ways in the respective countries.

Poland has recently adopted a predominantly welfare orientated model for dealing with minors (those under 17), with the introduction of family courts in 1978, and the Acts of October 1982. Whilst this is regarded as a modern and progressive trend in Poland, England is moving back to a justice based model. The 1982 Criminal Justice Act introduced determinate sentencing for young offenders, with fewer distinctions between adults and juveniles. The stricter experimental regimes in detention centres introduced in 1979 have now been extended to all detention centres. The notion of the rehabilitative aspects of custodial provisions have largely been abandoned, as symbolised by the return to the wearing of uniform by youth custody staff. Although the Act has simultaneously emphasised preventative, community based approaches, this seems to have made little impact on the total numbers in custody. Whilst detention centre sentences have decreased by 16 per cent, and the use of custody by 5 per cent, youth custody has risen by 41 per cent since the introduction of the Act.

There appear to be two strands behind this change of direction in England, the first being a more punitive climate of opinion particularly in respect of young offenders, and the second being the apparent failure of the welfare approach as embodied in the 1969 Children and Young Persons Act. This Act has had the unintended consequence of ultimately increasing the number of young offenders in custody, or at least, failing in its intention to achieve any reduction, and increasing the use of restrictive and punitive measures (Rutter and Giller, 1983). However, many of the more radical provisions in the 1969 Act were never implemented and the principles of justice and welfare were left to compete in an uneasy balance. Welfare principles had the effect of 'net widening', drawing in young people with social need rather than gravity of offence alone. Sentencing according to justice principles escalated their progression on the tariff into care and custody leading to disillusionment with the welfare model at various levels.

There may, however, be different factors in operation in Poland which will militate against a similar 'failure' of welfare intervention. The negative consequences of institutional life have been acknowledged in Poland: the effectiveness of reformatories in the field of resocialisation has been doubtful for many years (Pykta, 1985). Ziemska also refers to doubts about the effectiveness of Children's Homes in socialising children (Ziemska, 1978). Any legislation, therefore, that results in an increasing number of young people in institutions in Poland would require careful scrutiny. In this context it may be helpful to note an apparent disparity in Poland between the treatment of young offenders and those over 25 and it may be that deviance is not regarded as serious until young people reach a certain age and are no longer under the control of their parents.

The characteristics of the justice model include the concept of offending as the result of individual choice and consequently, personal responsibility for one's actions. Proof of guilt is required before intervention and punishment take place. The relevance of the adversarial system of law is assumed, and offences and sanctions should be clearly defined in Law. 'Just deserts' or 'tariff' sentencing is regarded by some legal opinion as a fashionable and proper approach today, because it promotes consistency between one offender and another, and reflects parliamentary and public feeling (Samuels, 1985).

The welfare model predominates in the field of juvenile offenders, and in England predates the 1969 Children and Young Persons Act, as the 1908 Children's Act also refers to the child's welfare. It is characterised by linking criminal activity with various disadvantages, with the aim of alleviating disadvantage, rather than punishing the offender.

The guilt of the offender is minimised, acknowledging some lack of control over circumstances. There is little distinction between offender and non-offender, as both are seen as having basically similar social needs. Tutt links the welfare with the medical model, which may focus on areas not directly related to offending (Tutt, 1983). Decision-making is discretionary and may result in indeterminate sentencing, which depends on the individual's response to 'treatment'.

Paradoxically, voluntary treatment may be overtaken by compulsion if this is judged to be in the individual's best interests or those of the public. This may have results as coercive as a justice based intervention.

Tutt also notes that no criminal justice system operates a pure model and that some compromise is often achieved. The Black Committee (1970) considered that the arrangements in England for dealing with juvenile offenders resulted in an accommodation of differing ideologies (Rutter and Giller, 1983). The combination of diversion and cautionary schemes in a justice model illustrates this accommodation.

In comparing England and Poland, it is relevant to identify how differing ideologies are balanced. Juvenile offence proceedings in Poland dropped from 60,000 to 30,000 between 1976 and 1982. Young people under 21 constitute one quarter of all persons sentenced and 26.5 per cent of the population is under 15. The state is concentrating resources on young people with the aim of further reducing this number. This reduction can also be partially explained by changes in legislation, transferring certain offences to the category of administrative transgressions, tried by special local committees. In 1966 and 1971 respectively 45,000 and 75,000 proceedings were moved to this category (Moskiciskier, 1985). Alcohol and drug abuse is also an area of concern in Poland. It has been estimated that 50 per cent of 14 year olds and 80 per cent of 15 - 18 year olds drink alcohol and treatment facilities have been expanded to cope with these problems which seem to be seen in the category of illness rather than crime. The 1982 Act introduced compulsory treatment for people with alcohol problems of up to two years, under the supervision of a probation officer. Many patients in treatment for drug addiction are under 16 and it is estimated that there may be 30,000 young heroin addicts in Poland (Ziemska, 1978).

The Polish Act of 1982 stated that the welfare of the minor was the main consideration in dealing with young offenders, and the transformation of Juvenile Courts to Family Courts was seen as an important part in this process. Family courts were set up in 1978, following earlier experiments in 1976. Prior to this, juveniles were dealt with in minors' courts, which also considered adult penal matters relating to the family. Judges were not trained specifically in family matters until 1978.

The laws relating to minors is based on the principle that the primary educational duty lies with parents. The family in Poland is regarded as the basic unit of society and has been described as one of the most vibrant forces holding the nation together (Steven, 1982). Historically, the partitioning of

Poland in the eighteenth century emphasised the role of the family in keeping the Polish identity alive, mainly through the education of children in language and culture by their mothers. The massive loss of life during World War II also seems to have made Poland more determined to rebuild the family as an institution as 22.3 per cent of the nation's children were left without parents (Ziemska, 1978). The emphasis on strengthening the care and educative functions of the family embodied in the 1982 Act is consistent with the view of the Roman Catholic Church, which has a powerful influence in Poland. The importance of child-rearing is given special attention, as reflected in the constitution of the Polish People's Republic and the Family and Guardianship Code and although Polish family law was influenced by Soviet legislation it showed a certain independence in the field of parent and child - Marriage, motherhood and family are in the care and protection of the Polish People's Republic (Ziemska, 1978).

The codified, justice based system of law in Poland would appear to be in conflict with the principles of a welfare approach. However, accommodations have been made within the code. The concept of 'social danger' allows for flexibility in the interpretation of the code, although 'social danger' has no precise legal definition. Decisions as to whether to prosecute, the defining of an act as an offence, the outcome of court proceedings and sentence length can depend on discretionary judgments as to whether an act constitutes a significant threat to social order, which lends itself to a political interpretation.

The 'intentionality' of an offence can also determine the length of sentence. Punishment can be more severe if it can be proved the offender could have foreseen the consequences. The concept of 'demoralisation' leads to a lack of distinction between offender and non-offender. It also has no precise legal definition and is related more to the needs of the offender than the offence itself. Decision making can therefore be discretionary, with lack of clarity or possible sanctions and indeterminate 'treatment' plans. Release from institutions depends on the young person's response to the institutional regime. Minors can be sent to Houses of Correction or homes with education, for offending or 'showing signs of demoralisation'. Demoralisation includes breaches of social conduct and association with criminal groups. Acts of 'hooligan character' are defined as 'showing disregard for basic principles of law and order' - concepts which are capable of being widely interpreted.

The ethos in relation to minors seems to be that offending and anti-social conduct is the consequence of an imperfect or incomplete socialisation process, requiring correction or redirection of attitudes and behaviour. This, in turn, implies some agreement on what constitutes existing social order. Offending by young people does not appear to be regarded as a direct challenge to norms and values or a real threat to law and order, in contrast to England, where it has been stated that concern over crime and inner city violence has raised a new wave of public anxiety about law and order, which is now regarded by voters as the second most important issue after unemployment. In 1984, law and order ranked only sixth in the list of problems facing the country.

The link with deviancy and disadvantage does not seem to be made in Poland. In theory, there are no significant disadvantages in socialist countries. Class differences are said to a large extent to have been obliterated and the principle of equal opportunity for all citizens has largely been established. However, over 30 per cent of Polish people are dependent on welfare benefits for survival (Schoflin, 1985). In contrast, delinquent behaviour in England is regarded by 'law and order' proponents as the expression of innate criminality. Social conditions are not considered to be linked to criminality and faulty socialisation processes are related to lack of discipline, rather than to the educational role of the family in its more general sense. The response to delinquency is therefore seen in terms of more deterrent sentencing for the majority of offenders designated 'depraved'. Although opposing views are expressed, linking occurrences of rioting, crime and violent behaviour to social conditions and environments, current public opinion seems to favour the former view, and rejects information which conflicts with this ideology.

Poland appears to steer a middle course by placing responsibility for delinquency firmly within the family. This minimises the effects of social conditions, whilst retaining a belief in the capacity of young people to respond to education and resocialising methods. Ziemska makes the link between education and delinquency clear when she states the inducement of desirable parental attitudes should contribute to the prevention of emotional disorders and eventually to the lowering of juvenile delinquency (Ziemska, 1978). This view allows little interpretation of deviance as having any meaning as an act of protest, a response to social conditions or a total rejection of society's norms. Probation officers in Poland do not appear to receive any training in identifying wider social problems. They become involved in the care of the juvenile's education if the family has lost its educational influence or is unable to fulfill its educational functions. The 1982 Act also reinforces the role of the community in supporting welfare measures for young offenders. Social organisations and work places can also be asked to undertake responsibility for supervising minors, and public opinion is seen as being in line with legislation.

The removal of a child from the home environment is seen as a last resort (Ziemska, 1978). In community homes with education, an average of 30 per cent are delinquents (Nocon, 1982). Contact with families is discouraged and few children have home leave, as the importance of preventing young people drifting back to deprived family environments is stressed. Treatment is aimed at removal from disadvantage rather than punishment, although the resident may view this action as equally coercive. Houses of Correction take minors between 13 and 21. There is an emphasis on education and work training within small, relatively comfortable units, which are regarded as the inmates' home. These institutions are graded for various types of security and need, and home leave is possible in certain institutions.

The 1969 Children and Young Persons Act in England was intended to replace most custodial correction for juveniles by rehabilitative community programmes, and diversion from custody. There had been a steep rise in reported crime between the mid-fifties and sixties and various committees had reported with recommendations for dealing with young offenders. The Ingleby Committee (1960) recommend that the welfare of the juvenile should be the primary objective of the juvenile court. The existence of welfare needs seemed to be taken for granted in the social conditions of the time. The 1933 Act had previously stated that courts should have regard for the welfare of the child, but magistrates tended to disregard the offence and deal with the offender. As in Poland, post-war development of child care services and psychological theories led to a belief that offending could be socially cured. However, there was a contradiction in implementing a welfare philosophy under criminal jurisdiction, which led to the setting up of Ingleby in 1957. Its recommendation to raise the age for prosecution to 14, with welfare need the main objective for offenders below 14, was considered to be unacceptable to public opinion and the age was merely raised from 8 to 10.

The 1965 White Paper 'The Child, The Family and Young Offender' had proposed replacing courts with 'hearings', inviting parents and offering flexible treatment programmes. Yet again the proposals were 'killed off' by objections. This was followed by the 1968 White Paper 'Children in Trouble', proposing the abolition of penal sanctions for offenders under 14. However, in the face of opposition the government gave an undertaking not to raise the age from 10 without approval from both Houses of Parliament.

The 1969 Act, with its radical proposals ran into similar difficulties. On returning to power in 1970, the Conservative government would not implement the sections of the Act with which it disagreed. Borstals and Detention Centres were retained and certificates of unruliness were widely used by magistrates to overcome their impotence at being unable to send children to approved schools (Rutter and Giller, 1983). The 1969 Act had envisaged the Juvenile Court as a welfare providing agency. Delinquency was considered to be the result of family inadequacies and evidence of the need for help and guidance. Treatment was to be left to the discretion of the experts, with indefinite periods of care until the age of 18. However, there was an increase in the use of punitive and restrictive measures after the Act, in spite of the fact that offending had peaked in 1972 and was 10 per cent lower in 1983 than in 1974. Diversion was not effective as care orders were being made before community based interventions were attempted. The effect was one of 'net widening' with a progression through the 'tariff'. Boundaries between freedom and captivity lost their clarity and a wider spectrum was drawn into the control system (Cohen, 1979). Although the reality of progression through the tariff is not formally acknowledged in law, there is evidence of its operation in the criminal justice systems following early social work intervention. The process usually accelerates the offender towards a higher degree of intervention by social work agencies if that young person is in court again for a further offence. If the offender is then seen as failing to respond, he is more likely to receive a custodial sentence.

The operation of the tariff in England may depend heavily on perceived public opinion, as magistrates are expected to act as representatives of the community in passing sentence. Whilst the tariff exists in the codified legal system in Poland, and flagrant and persistent infringement of regulations can result in a sentence of deprivation of liberty, there is more emphasis on looking at the needs of the offender, rather than the offence, as the main consideration. Tariff sentencing would appear to operate for adults although it is not clear where an adult with previous convictions as a juvenile would enter the tariff.

Dicey and Walker have emphasised the dependence of law on public opinion (Dicey, 1962; Walker, 1982) and there is evidence in Europe and the USA of the 'resurgence of just deserts' as the dominant penal philosophy, in response to the public mood on sentencing, although in Scotland there is no significant public reaction to an innovative welfare approach: Manchester considers that the Scots are not interested in tariffs (Manchester, 1985).

The English media appears preoccupied with the theme of law and order, whereas the main focus in Poland has been on the economic and political situation. The main function of newspapers in Poland is to convey state views and policies, although their degree of openness varies. Law and order is not a main feature and individual crimes are rarely reported. The exception to this generalisation has been noted by some Western writes (Ruane, 1982). Crimes seemed to be reported in detail when the state wished to draw attention away from the economic situation. At one time, court results were published, but this has now been discontinued, apparently on economic grounds. It was not clear whether this was because crime had increased. However, when Solidarity became active in 1980 in the press, on radio and TV alarming crime statistics were produced seemingly pointing to a virtual collapse of law and order, which linked crime with Solidarity. In May 1980, there were a number of violent incidents in Warsaw, including football hooliganism and arson. Ruane considered the most remarkable thing was that the incidents were given so much publicity and that law and order became a big political issue, with the State Council describing a growth of criminology unheard of hitherto, trying to threaten the function of the state. However, there was apparent public scepticism about the reported rise in crime and demands for firmer action appearing in the press. Public mistrust of the police and the lack of an obvious link between hooliganism and Solidarity were said to have contributed to this scepticism.

Public opinion in Poland may have affected sentencing for certain types of crime. The penalty for rape was increased from three to ten years, as the stated result of police opinion, and theft of cars is regarded as a serious offence, reflecting the difficulty in obtaining one. However, thefts from employers and black market involvement, whilst regarded as crime by the state, are not seen in such a serious light by many Polish people. Pilfering from work places is described as happening on a gargantuan scale. In general, incidence of crime is similar to England in that offences against property predominate, with the majority of offenders under 20 (Mosciskier, 1985) and penalties for crimes of violence seem comparable to those in England.

The media in Britain appear to have a far more significant role in shaping public opinion, as there is more cynicism in Poland regarding the veracity of the media and its statements about how the public feel. Hall et al. consider the English media to be dominated by the primary definers of crime - the police, courts and Home Office, who hold a near monopoly on sources of crime news (Hall, 1978). There is a predominance of crime reporting in the press and crime, particularly violent crime, appears to be one of the most popular sections in newspapers (Jones, 1980). The main conclusions of the Report of the Council of Europe is that whilst experiences of crime played a limited role in the development of public attitudes, media portrayal of crime fed the punitive syndrome and counteracted efforts towards the resocialisation of delinquents. Retribution is also an important sentencing concept in England and is referred to by Hall as the punitive obsession. Hall describes the role of the daily press as assuming that the public voice thunders in the name of the people, for vengeance (Tutt, 1976). This punitive and retributive view is accepted across the classes in Britain, particularly among older people and manual workers. There is evidence that manual workers are more likely to be the victims of crime (Hough and Moxon, 1985).

The traditionalist consensus is said to be characterised by ideologies of respectability, the Protestant work ethic, concern about the breakdown of family life and the permissive society, and an emphasis on discipline and respect for law and order (Hall, 1978). These ideologies tend to result in a class consensus on crime, crudely encapsulated in a recent public lecture by a cabinet minister: the trigger of today's outburst of crime and violence lies in the era and attitudes of postwar funk which gave birth to the permissive society, which in turn, generated today's violent society. More punitive attitudes to young offenders in England are consistent with this view, as offenders can be categorised as depraved rather than deprived. Inner city riots during 1981 and 1984 seem to have led to a hardening of attitudes in England. Discipline, in terms of corporal punishment is still widespread in England, and is used in British schools. Indeed moves were made to reintroduce corporal punishment in the earlier stages of a Bill leading to the 1982 Criminal Justice Act.

In contrast, Poland's attitudes towards child-rearing practices in general have altered considerably since the 1950s with the influence of psychological and developmental theories. Ziemska describes post war child care as rigid, and lacking any emphasis on the parent/child bond. The norm is now one of encouragement and positive reinforcement. Although less educated parents are said to be more in favour of corporal punishment, the influence of the media and schools is one of disapproval of physical punishment with disciplinary sanctions enforced against staff who use if (Ziemska, 1978).

Extreme views on crime and punishment are thereby modified by ideological and practical considerations. In England, however, the dominant ideologies already described appear to gain support through media concentration on moral panics – issues of public concern with controversial factors – such as youth, drugs and hooliganism. Moral panics may then develop into general panics, culminating in law and order campaigns (Hall, 1978). Statistical and abstract analysis seem to lack the impact of retributive rhetoric and fail to offer any real challenge to the traditionalist consensus. Previous attempts to set maximum penalities by the Advisory Council have received hostile press treatment, in spite of the legal qualifications of the people involved (Jones, 1978). The British Crime Surveys of 1982 and 1984 indicate that whilst previous opinion polls appear to have revealed a punitive mood, victims of crime were less punitive than might have been anticipated. Moxon noted that both victims and sentencers share a belief in age as a mitigating factor in sentencing, with agreement on 25 year olds and over being sentenced more severely. The Crime Survey conclusion is that media claims about public opinion and more punitive treatment offenders can be treated with some scepticism by the courts and policy makers (Hough and Moxon, 1985).

Judges in England, however, still continue to take public opinion into account when sentencing, claiming at the same time independence in sentencing matters, because of the separation of powers between the legislature, executive and judiciary. In Poland, there is a direct line of responsibility from the state, through the Ministry of Justice to the judges. The state, in passing legislation, considers public opinion to have been taken into account fully and judges are expected to accept the ideology of the state when sentencing minors. Judges are specifically trained in family law to deploy prophylaxis and rehabilitation as well as supervising the execution of the courts' decisions (Stojanowska, 1985).

The theory of separation of powers is contradicted by the Office of Lord Chancellor who combines three functions as head of the legal profession, Minister of Justice and Speaker in the House of Lords. Even Lord Denning has acknowledged that the theory of a neutral judiciary is not matched by practice and that in criminal law, judges are as much concerned as the executive with the prosecution of law and order (Hall, 1978). Whilst the 'primary definers' influence both changes in legislation and public opinion in the media, it is perhaps hardly surprising that a more punitive response to young offenders is the result of a consensus between state legislation, sentencers and public opinion in England, whilst the consensus in Poland on dealing with minors seems to have moved in the opposite direction.

The consensus of opinion in Poland relates to a broad agreement about the role of the family and the responsibility of both the family and the community to socialise young people. The state, the church and the courts all seem to share a similar view on the primary importance of the family. The widespread debate on family life initiated in 1973 was encouraged in higher government circles, with a view to the emergence of new social legislation. Polish Family Law holds parents responsible for children, and parents can be fined for failing to fulfil parental duties. Even siblings are mutually responsible for each other's support and in this respect, the Polish code is unique (Wojiechowski, 1973).

Although resources have not kept pace with need, there is considerable state support for the family, as the state accepts responsibility for the complete development of young people, assisted by many social and voluntary agencies. There are services for children of working mothers, holiday camps for children, community day centres and ample creche and nursery facilities. The divorce rate in Poland has not increased at the same rate as in other European countries (Ziemska, 1985). The influence of the Catholic Church and difficulty in finding alternative accommodation may account for this situation to some extent but the ideology shared by most Polish people which considers the family, not the individual, as the basic social unit has been an equally important influence.

The institution of the family in England, by contrast, seems to be under more pressure, with one in three marriages ending in divorce and increasing numbers of one parent families living at minimal income levels. In 1976, approximately 10 per cent of families with dependent children were headed by single parents. Townsend has estimated 26 per cent of the population as living in poverty with a further 25 per cent on the margin of the state's poverty line. Children and the elderly are the largest groups affected by poverty. Amongst the low paid, those with children are most likely to be in poverty.

Resources are not devoted to supporting the family structure in England, although breakdown of the family is regarded as a contributory factor in offending. The importance of the family is often referred to in a negative sense, with the lessening of a firm and stable family life for children and lack of home and school discipline perceived as contributing to a breakdown of law and order. This ambivalence towards the institution of the family is also reflected in ambivalence towards young offenders. Whilst children have been accepted as incapable of criminal responsibility as a social category, modifications of the 1969 Act were aimed at removing the dominance of this welfare orientation. When the 1969 Act was only partially implemented in 1970 the courts sentenced in a way which was clearly against the philosophy and spirit of the Act (Hall, 1978). Additionally, resources to implement existing sections of the Act were not forthcoming and schemes such as intermediate treatment were required to operate at minimal cost until 1983.

It is therefore difficult to argue that the welfare approach 'failed', when it was never fully implemented. Sentencing continued on the basis of the tariff, rather than individual need, encouraged by media presentation of views on law and order. Disillusionment with the welfare model seemed to be shared by magistrates, social workers and academics alike, opening the way for a return to a justice model. Ambivalence towards young offenders has been retained, however, in the concept of diversion from custody for less serious offences, or for offenders who can respond to community supervision and pehaps be categorised as deprived. At the same time, punitive detention centre regimes have been retained and youth imprisonment – Youth Custody – extended.

In Poland, general agreement on the role of the family and the responsibility of the community and the state for young people seems to lead to a greater commitment to the welfare of the minor as a priority when sentencing. However, there is evidence that a substantial proportion of young people are in institutional care, although the number of Houses of Correction has fallen, with twelve being closed in recent years (Nocon, 1982). In 1983, there were 464 young offenders in educational establishments, 2,515 in Correctional Schools and 2,549 in Houses of Correction (5,528 or 15.3 per cent of offenders under 18) (Bielen, 1985). In England, in 1983, 12 per cent of young offenders between 14 and 16 were given custodial sentences. 5,710 received Detention Centre sentences and 6,910 Youth Custody (12,620) (NACRO, 1985). In England there are 31 Youth Custody Centres, 19 Detention Centres and 5 Remand Centres, dealing solely with offenders, whereas in Poland there are 29 Houses of Correction, 49 Youth Education Centres (taking a proportion of offenders) and 21 Remand Homes.

These figures are not directly comparable because of a number of variables, including youth custody sentencing to the age of 20, but give some indication of the place of institutional care in sentencing in the respective countries (both England and Poland take children into care, where offending is also involved, but these figures do not include this category).

In general terms, therefore, Poland has 99 establishments

dealing with offenders, compared to 55 in England. Institutions in Poland are run on family lines and seem to be regarded as state substitutes for families who are unable to offer adequate socialisation to their children whilst the primary aim of institutions in England is punishment.

Research evidence on institutional care would suggest that the regimes for young offenders in Poland are more likely to be successful than young offender regimes in England. It has been recognised in Poland that reconviction rates are higher for young offenders who have been confined in closed institutions than for those who received open sentences (Nocon, 1982).

Success rates following institutional care in a number of countries, as assessed by reconviction rates are generally poor with a 60 - 70 per cent failure rate. However, this may be more of a reflection of the types of offender or the quality of the institution. Giller and Rutter summarise the main findings in this area from a number of countries, which show that institutions can have a substantial effect on young people during their stay and the characteristics of the more successful institutions are stated as a combination of firmness, warmth, harmony, high expectations, good discipline and a practical approach to training (Rutter and Giller, 1983). Pending research into the long term outcomes and comparative studies, these authors suggest it would be sensible to run institutional regimes along these lines, paying equal attention to the environment to which the young person will be returning. Houses of Correction operate on the basis of replicating the atmosphere of a family and even regimes for difficult offenders are said to be less rigid than most homes (Nocon, 1982). The training programmes are relevant to work which will be available outside the institution and Community Homes with education also provide work and training in small family groups until the age of 18.

Greater attention has now been given to the after care of young offenders released from institutions in Poland. Previously limited powers were extended by the 1982 Act and legislative powers in 1983, when a separate system for dealing with minors was instituted. Prior to this, minors were dealt with under the adult system of post penitentiary aid. The aim is to prevent recidivism amongst demoralised minors (Piechowiak, 1985). The duties of the probation officer include finding accommodation, work, training and various forms of aid. This is particularly important when young offenders are released from institutions some considerable distance from their homes and in cases where a return to a poor home environment is actively discouraged.

Whilst institutional care is seen as an acceptable form of state welfare provision for both offenders and non-offenders, with efforts being directed towards maintaining a family type environment, there is also an awareness of the need for it to be seen as a last resort, in view of the possibility of negative consequences. There still appears to be a danger of 'net widening' operating in Poland unless community based supervision is expanded.

Patterns of offending by young people in Poland and England have clear similarities in terms of peak ages for offending and the predominance of certain crimes and although their stated sentencing philosophy is very different, both societies still have substantial numbers of young people in institutions. While the justice/welfare debate has been criticised for its sterility in terms of its capacity to generate new insights or programmes for action (Raynor, 1985), it does provide a framework for examining the respective values behind the juvenile justice systems in these two countries. It would appear that both societies are as much influenced by ideological values as statistical information and research. Changes in legislation and recategorisation of offences could be equally responsible for changes in crime rates for young people in both countries, but little research evidence linking family inadequacy in socialising young people with delinquency was presented on the exchange visit to Poland to support this strongly held belief.

Law and order is an issue strongly associated with the media and party politics in England and highly susceptible to swings in legislative trends. The Conservative party is currently seen as the party best able to deal with law and order, in spite of a large recorded increase in crime during their term of office and the belief in the effectiveness of more punitive sentencing seems to have been maintained. Both England and Poland have shown a tendency to criminalise behaviour seen to threaten the order of the state, as indicated by the introduction in response to rioting and strikes of a public order act in England and declarations of martial law in Poland. Both societies also seem to respond pragmatically to rising prison populations. Poland dealt with the situation by declaring an amnesty, whilst England extended the use of parole which was regarded by some sentencers as a 'back door' method of reducing prison populations, without appearing to reduce sentence lengths [1].

Although the justice model has so far been unsuccessful in reducing numbers in youth custody, there is little evidence of public concern. Rutter and Giller consider that society must decide for itself the social purposes and values it considers most important, in order to establish a balance between justice and welfare principles. The complex interaction of empirical evidence, ideology and politics and media influence can result in extremes which are equally coercive and ineffective. The absence of a consistent sentencing principle resulting from conflicting principles, leads to very arbitrary justice (Gibson, 1985).

Total commitment to particular ideologies may serve the function of providing a society with a sense of security and purpose, but does not further understanding of the complex phenomenon of crime, or lead to more objective evaluations of alternative views of the effectiveness of crime prevention, legislation and sentencing. Rutter and Giller illustrate this limitation. Criminologists express a view about society and about human behaviour which is extended to criminality. Accordingly, the main limitation of criminological theories lie in their failure to deal with, or notice some of the most striking empirical findings (Rutter and Giller, 1983). In this context, perceptions of justice and welfare in both countries seem to provide a rationale for a more selective and biased interpretation of offending, rather than a genuine attempt to understand its complexity.

Notes

[1] Poland's population is 37 million, with 83,000 prisoners (368 are political prisoners).
England has a population of 56 million with 48,000 prisoners.
The Prosecutor-General of Poland will consider the release of political prisoners (Guardian 13 November 1985).
England extended the use of parole in 1983 to prisoners serving sentences in excess of ten and a half months.
Poland also released considerable numbers of prisoners in 1983, reducing numbers from over 100,000.

4 Justice for the family

MARTIN CHANCE

Abstract

A comparative study of the Polish Family Court and the Legal
System dealing with families and children in England and Wales.
The study deals with the very wide differences in practice and
procedure which exists between Poland and England in relation
to the family when it finds itself in contact with the law,
whether civil or ciminal.   I will attempt to compare the
Polish Family Court with similar legal structures in England
and Wales.   Although a Family Court system does not operate in
England, such proposals have been talked about in the Courts,
Committees, and Parliament for the last thirty years, but there
is still little sign of a Family Court emerging within the
foreseeable future.   Finally I will make comment on the
failure to implement these proposals and hope to offer some
insight as to why the various reports have not been adopted.

* * * * *

The Polish nation, despite severe setbacks over the past two
hundred years is resilient and its peoples have a history of
surviving against all the odds. There have been wars, economic
disasters and political unrest but despite all difficulties the

54

family emerges as being as strong and resolute as ever, providing a framework for the future wellbeing of the nation. During World War II the three generation family became the essential institution of national organisation in the resistance and underground struggle (Szczepanski, 1970). Post war reconstruction has had significant consequences for family life due to mass migration, industrialisation and equality for women. Since 1945 legal protection, health care, education and social services have developed rapidly (Ziemska, 1975). In Poland grandparents continue to play an important role within the family circle (Halecki, 1978). During the war grandparents stayed in their own locality to provide a link and offer stability, despite the fact that it would have been safer to have moved away from intensive hostilities. Adam Nickiewicz, the Polish national poet said that the birth place will always be sacred and pure as first love. In England, the family is regarded as being important but is not so closely knit as in Poland.

How did the Polish Family Court begin? Why Family Courts? The concept of Family Courts was based on the assumption that the protection and strengthening of the family as the basic unit of society was, in essence, necessary for the development of the whole country. In Poland it was widely accepted that an individual was answerable to the whole nation, but, in return, relied on the family to strengthen that resolve.

The preparation for Family Courts appeared in the early 1960s with the creation of separate family sections in Katowice in 1962 and in Lodz in 1963 (Stojanowska, 1985). In these courts, divorce, paternity, alimony and property disputes between spouses were dealt with. No great movement had taken place but this gave the authority to plan and research for further work. At this time all other matters were dealt with by the District Courts which resemble the Magistrates Courts in England today.

The next phase of the system took place between 1974 and 1975 when family sections in ten courts operated on experimental principles, different from those of Katowice and Lodz. The results of research showed that the Family Courts which had operated in an experimental way had not functioned according to earlier intentions. Research showed that there was a likelihood of juvenile offenders under guardianship matters being neglected in favour of other civil matters regulated by the family and guardianship code of 1964. This is an important finding for the English system to note if it seeks to combine juvenile and civil court functions in a Family Court.

The research noted the lack of professional qualifications of some judges who dealt with both penal and civil matters. There was a similar lack of properly trained auxiliary staff within the courts in the experimental areas. In 1976 the Department of Family Minors' Affairs of the Ministry of Justice was charged with the leadership of further development of jurisdiction in family mattrs. The earlier experience of focussing on family matters paved the way for creation of new courts and prepared the ground for a far reaching reform of a system of justice in 1978.

Discussion among government departments, lawyers, judges and the general public led to an early decision being made to develop Family Courts across most of Poland. On 1 January 1978 family and juvenile sections, called Family Courts, were created at District Court level (the lower court in Poland). The whole of Poland was not covered, but in those areas where a Family Court had been constituted, selected judges were appointed to deal with family matters. Juvenile offenders who had previously been dealt with in a separate court, were now dealt with under the jurisdiction of the Family Court.

By October 1982 the whole of Poland had been incorporated within a system to deal with family matters. Initially a Family Court, in dealing with divorce matters, also dealt with the property aspect of the marriage, but this is now dealt with following the making of the divorce absolute. This is not so in England, a point which will be discussed later. The Polish authorities, in reaching this decision, felt that the question of debating property rights which could be complex, often delayed the divorce proceedings, leaving the family in limbo. Here again, is an example of putting the family issues first and accepting the fundamental values of family life.

The Polish model is impressive because the working situation is closer and the Polish probation officer may be more professional than he realises or accepts. Since the arrival of the Family Court, juvenile crime in Poland has been halved. Could this be the influence of the court and its advisers working in close harmony for the benefit of families and the community?

The Polish legal system differs considerably from that in England and on first examination the Polish system could be considered more precise and within codified principles. The court structure which includes the Family Court, is based on a tiered structure similar to the English system, but that is where the parallel ends. While the rule of law is necessary both in Poland and England and its maintenance paramount, the Polish people regard law breaking as against the fabric of society. There are, however, grave questions waiting to be asked regarding human rights and freedom of speech.

In Poland the courts are:

a) <u>Supreme Court</u> - dealing with affairs of state, appeals from the Voivoidship (an administrative area resembling an English County Court) and questions of law. This court is very similar to the English High Court (Court of Appeal and Family Division) dealing with criminal and civil matters.

b) <u>Voivoidship Court</u> - presided over by judges dealing with serious offences and acting as the Appeal Court for the District Court. Once again, this court is similar in structure and function to the English Crown Court. The English Crown Court deals with serious cases and acts as an Appeal Court from Magistrates.

c) <u>District Court</u> - this is the lowest court in Poland and is presided over by judges and lay assessors. This court can be compared with the English Magistrates Court and the Juvenile Court.

All matters of a civil nature in Poland are dealt with within district institutions of various tiers and there are therefore no parallels in the English County Courts which exist solely for civil matters dealing with affairs of property, finance and divorce. The Family Court in Poland, as such, exists in all tiers and deals with young offenders covered by the English Juvenile Court.

Judges preside in all Polish courts and are accountable directly to the state which is indicative of the authority of the state over its peoples. This is in strict contrast to the English system where 95 per cent of all legal work is undertaken by lay magistrates who are appointed to serve the community from the community.

The Polish judges must qualify as lawyers and attend two years' professional training before being appointed. Family Court judges may not be appointed under the age of thirty and have considerable experience and working knowledge of families. In District Courts two lay assessors sit with the judge, they are appointed from persons of good standing in the community and sit for four years. In England, it is only in the Crown Courts that lay persons sit with a judge.

One of the major criticisms of English magistrates dealing with family and juvenile matters is the lack of experience, continuity and opportunities to gain more knowledge of welfare and criminal matters (Cavenagh, 1962). They do, however, receive professional assistance from Justices' Clerks, who in the main are legally qualified and influential. In Poland the judge is the authority in his, or more frequently her, own right. The qualities which are needed in every magistrate who sits in a Juvenile Court are a love of young people, sympathy with their rights, and imaginative insight into their difficulties. The rest is largely common sense (Halecki, 1978).

English magistrates in Juvenile Courts are required to retire from the Bench at the age of 65 but they may return to the courts to deal with domestic matters until they reach the age of 70. Magistrates in England are appointed by the Lord Chancellor's Department and work to rules laid down by the Home Secretary. Initially, magistrates are interviewed by a local committee. They come from various walks of life and one of the criticisms laid against them is that they are not representative of the local community and may not even live in the vicinity of the court where they sit. Magistrates in England are not legally qualified and serve in a voluntary capacity for a limited number of half-days per month.

The Family Court in Poland, with its various divisions, deals with all matters affecting the family, whereas in England family matters as such are dealt with by various courts. It came as no surprise to learn from Polish friends that they had difficulty in comprehending the various courts in England and their functions in relation to young people which I set out below:

a) <u>Juvenile Court</u> - deals with juvenile offenders between the ages of 10 and 17 years, some adoptions of children and care proceedings.

b) <u>Magistrates' Court</u> - may deal with juveniles when appearing with adults; the court acts in relation to domestic proceedings involving husband and wife.

c) <u>County Court</u> - deals with adoptions and divorce matters as well as other civil matters relating to property and finance.

d) <u>Crown Court</u> - may deal with juveniles on serious charges and act as an Appeal Court to the Juvenile Court. The Court of Appeal and Family Division may also deal with complicated family matters. The system is regarded as a complex one which will be discussed further, later.

In the Polish District Court a judge is appointed to a local area comprising 35,000 people and will have direct knowledge of a locality and its varying problems. In addition the curator (probation officer) works closely to the judge. This system allows the curator and judge to work together as a team with obvious advantages to the family, the offender and community. One criticism may be that the judge will invariably see people who make a habit of breaking the law. But the same may happen in England where people appear before the local court where it is common practice for habitual offenders to seek trial by jury or at least to be sentenced by the judge of the Crown Court in the hope of being dealt with impartially.

With the English system, some magistrates are not particularly interested in the probation service. It is evident that some magistrates do not have a particularly good knowledge of the locality, perhaps resulting from their living a considerable distance from their court area. Quarterly meetings between magistrates and probation officers are held to review cases. These meetings may be attended by only a small group of magistrates who show interest in the social work side of their duties.

The divorce rate in Poland is not so high as in England, but divorce proceedings are slowly on the increase (Ziemska, 1985). In any society parents and children experience failure, disturbance and suffering caused by the break up of a marriage. Often divorce itself is rather tempestuous and the decision to divorce may be preceded by a period of tension. The work of the Family Court is concerned with divorce, conciliation and reconciliation. The Poles have a less legalistic framework than the English, with parties appearing before the judge who has the role of investigator and conciliator. The judge interviews the husband and wife separately and at the initial stages they are not represented.

In England both parties may be legally represented and this situation can result in difficulties with either legal advisor setting out to win the case for their client, sometimes with little thought for the real welfare of the children. The Polish judge will only make a divorce absolute if satisfied that the children will not suffer. In some situations the judge will not grant a divorce and both parties may continue to live under the same roof, although effectively the marriage is finished. In other cases a divorce may be granted but the father or mother continue to live in the same house because of the acute housing shortage.

One senses that divorce is not so easily obtainable in Poland as it is in England. In England divorcees are given greater assistance with financial and housing difficulties than hitherto and divorce is no longer regarded as a social stigma. In Poland it is usually the wife or mother who experiences the most difficulty and, as stated previously, seeking rehousing causes many problems.

However, divorce in Poland is only undertaken after much has been done to save the marriage. The Roman Catholic church plays an important part in the preservation of the sanctity of marriage and has agencies for assisting families. The probation service in Poland is used by the Family Court much as in England where the Divorce Court Welfare Officer is appointed by the local probation service.

The Polish judge clearly has more authority within the divorce situation than an English counterpart and is able to decide whether a marriage has broken down permanently. Special reports may be requested on the children or family in both countries, but in Poland, Family Diagnostic Units, attached to the court, will provide back up informaton. This service is unique and will be discussed further. Supervision can be ordered in both countries but, unlike in England where the children are named, in Poland the orders are to include the whole family which, again, places the emphasis on the importance of the family unit. Additionally, in Poland supervision may be undertaken by a social or voluntary guardian as well as the professional probation officer.

It is said that the supervisors in Poland do not have to contend with such a high degree of emotional intensity as in England. This factor could be the result of the amount of personal responsibility that the state places on individuals as well as the family and parents, before deciding a divorce.

The practice of conciliation can be an integral part of the divorce proceedings both in Poland and England with conciliation focussed on assisting the parties to deal with the consequences of the breakdown of their marriage by reaching agreements or giving consents (Harper, 1982), reducing the areas of conflict over custody, support and access to children, financial position, disposition of the matrimonial home and other matters arising from the breakdown.

The way conciliation is practised by the Polish Family Court demands that formal procedures are established and these include work by the curator or social guardian, as well as staff of the diagnostic centres. Conciliation is also undertaken by voluntary agencies but the main Polish system is focussed through the Polish structure.

In England conciliation has been rather slow in gathering momentum. In some areas probation service voluntary schemes have been undertaken and in others the service is available to all comers and not restricted to a court organisation. In England recommendation for the setting up of a national conciliation scheme have not been taken up and insufficient funding has been available for staff and training.

The provisions of the Polish Centres for Counselling and Diagnosis originated in 1967, at which stage they dealt with criminal cases (Siedlecka, 1985). Previously very many young people had been committed to chidren's units and prison type establishments without having the benefit of special and professional reports. Many children were sent to unsuitable institutions to be discovered shortly afterwards as misplaced and suffering from mental illness or emotional disturbance; hence the establishment of special centres to provide observation and detailed personality studies.

Existing centres such as health clinics, children's homes and educational counselling centres were used. In 1966 the Ministry of Justice examined the system and found that too many children were being sent away from home unnecessarily. By 1974 some twenty diagnostic centres were set up in Poland and regualtions brought into force under the responsibility of the Ministry of Justice. These regulations gave courts the opportunity, in principle, to examine every child appearing before the court. As a result, judges began to benefit considerably from the expert advice given in written reports.

In 1978 when the Family Courts in Poland were set up, Family Counselling Centres were introduced, usually attached to Family Courts or to centres where young people were sent for observation. Initially cases involved criminal activity but soon involved all Family Court matters.

Staff based at the centres include psychiatrists, doctors, psychologists, educational advisers and social counsellors. The role of the centre is comprehensive and the aims are as follows:

1. To conduct psychological, social, educational, medical and community studies, as well as forming an opinion about children, their parents or guardians.

2. To run family counselling and provide care.

3. To assist the state institutions and social organisations in dealing with difficult cases and protect the family, and the prevention of social breakdown of children.

In addition, the centres provide specialist guidance to children under supervision, transfer of cases to other specialist agencies and provide specialist counselling in support of probation officers.

The reports on children and parents are submitted to the judge and most bear the signatures of three centre staff to show their agreement with the observations and recommendations.

These counselling and diagnostic centres may be compared with child guidance clinics in England which operate under the auspices of the local authority education and social services departments but are removed from the Juvenile Courts. From personal observation, the Polish centres have a much better professial adaptation to the needs of the court and of children appearing in the Family Court than their English counterparts. It was therefore apparent to me that the Polish system, being court based, had considerable advantages over the English system, particularly in respect of the children of divorcing couples. Child guidance clinics deal with remedial and preventative cases but not specifically with the needs of children in divorce as such, unless there is a medical referral.

Diagnostic work will be undertaken by an English social services department if the child is placed in a special observation centre, but this usually requires the child to be placed away from home for the assessment period. One interesting feature of the Polish system is that treatment plans following diagnosis will be introduced, whether the child returns home or is placed elsewhere. One can well argue that the Polish system has much to commend it and I am aware that the services are highly valued by the Family Court judges.

Whilst the historical foundations of the court systems are similar in both countries, it appeared easier for Poland within a codified legal system to set up Family Courts. The system was organised after five years of deliberations and proposals, but without having to confront the kind of obstacles presented by the very complicated legal and social machinery that exists in England.

Criticisms of the Polish Family Court system appear to be few and relate to the internal procedure policies, rather than opposition to the concept of family justice within a system of codified laws. The welfare service to the state courts is provided singularly by curators who have additional responsibilities to those of their English counterparts in that they undertake care and control proceedings of young people and there is no doubt that justice for the family remains paramount.

Why did it take so long for Family Courts to be seriously considered in England? The family is an important unit for the wellbeing of the country but responsibility is placed on the parents for the upbringing of the children has been submerged during the past thirty years in preoccupations about criminality. Less attention has been paid to the orgins of criminality in poor housing, poverty, low education and attainments, and unemployment.

In this context the question of whether to include the Juvenile Courts within a wider ambit of Family Courts have been variably examined by numerous committees and individuals, many of whom agree that the Juvenile Court should remain separate so as not to merge welfare matters with criminal sentencing (Hall, 1970). One thing is certain, most committees see the need to reorganise the Juvenile Court (Morris, 1981). There is, however, much to commend the use of experienced family magistrates dealing with domestic, juvenile and criminal proceedings.

The question for more effective training for magistrates has arisen and it is generally felt that they should undergo regular training and have access to discussion groups. At the same time, judges should possess a broad knowledge of the various welfare services available to families in stress. In 1965 the White Paper 'The Child, The Family and The Young Offender' foresaw Family Courts as dealing primarily with delinquency. In 1968 during a debate on the Report of the Committee for Local Authority Allied Personal Social Services, which was concerned with the reorganisation of social service departments, it was said that the present services were fragmented and unco-ordinated. It was considered that overall requirements of neither the individual nor family were being met (Bryant, 1981).

The probation service, wishing to retain its separate identity and backed by the Magistrates' Association, fought hard successfully to avoid inclusion in the reorganisation of the social services, even though its stance created ambiguities (Murch, 1980). I personally feel this was a professional blunder and one which society will come to regret. Both the social services and the probation service continued to overlap their services in dealing with divorce, adoption, family matters and juvenile offenders at a time when resources are stretched. I contend that this is a matter for renewed scrutiny, being one of the major obstacles to change in making proper provision for the family.

The Children and Young Persons Act 1969 did very little to assist in the matter of providing a better deal for young children. The legal profession, whilst seen to be making the right noises about reform, have tended to be half-hearted in their support. A committee sat for four years considering proposals jointly with the Home Office, which were then suspended when it was realised that the Finer Report on the needs of the one parent family was likely to recommend the foundation of Family Courts. The Report was finally published and it strongly advocated Family Courts and made specific recommendations for a separate social work service. It suggested that finance need not be a burden nor a stumbling block to the implementation of its proposals. Regrettably successive governments have seen that Family Courts would be a heavy financial commitment for the Exchequer and rejected the proposal on those grounds. When the report was debated in the House of Commons the then Secretary of State for Social Services, Barbara Castle, concluded by saying (even though the Labour Party Manifesto contained a commitment to the principle of providing Family Courts) that the government could see no prospect for accepting the recommendations for Family Courts.

By the end of the seventies it looked as though Family Courts would never be established in England. Politicians, lawyers and social anthropologists all conceded that the seventies was not the right period for the provision of such a far-reaching change. In other words, there were too many complexities: concerning training of judges, impact on lawyers, magistrates' fears of loss of domestic court work, resistance to the loss of the Juvenile Court, the role of the County Court. All these appeared as great problems. Then again, what role would social workers and probation officers play?

I believe that the full implementation of the Seebohm Report would have greatly eased the situation for the beginnings of a Family Court. The Home Office, whilst not pubicly opposing the probation service's involvement in civil work and to some extent juvenile work, does not support the service in attempting to obtain additional resources for such work, preferring the service to continue its endeavours in the crime prevention field.

Overlapping of work continues and the Lord Chancellor continues to make statements that a Family Court is necessary but does little or nothing to enable progress on changing the system to take place. A question remains unanswered – when will the family have justice? – I suspect not this century.

5 Militaristic aspects of a prison service — Poland/UK comparison

IVAN ZOBKIW

Abstract

As a result of an exercise in comparative studies, a group of
English probation officers were, in June 1985, able to sample
what can best be described as a Polish Experience.   Whilst in
its entirety this consisted of gaining an understanding of the
nature of Poland, its historical legacy of occupation and
suffering and its people, particular professional interest lay
in the ability to observe at first hand, how another society,
especially one with a very different economic and political
base, reacted to similar problems arising from the fields of
delinquency and criminality - areas of concern that are
experienced in differing ways, and dealt with by all modern and
developed nations differently.

* * * * *

As part of this exercise, a colleague and myself spent one week
in the north west of Poland, in the administrative region or
Voivody of Bydgoscz, specifically to look at a number of
custodial establishments and their place within the criminal
justice system.   The area was chosen because of its high
density of custodial establishments, in an area which was

formerly Prussia.   During our stay in Poland some five Houses of Correction and a penitentiary were visited.

The establishments catered for juveniles and young offenders, the Houses of Correction catered for the 13-17 year age group, all of which operated with spare capacity, excellent staffing ratios, and staff dedicated to their task and role, and indeed methods used to effect resocialisation.

Uniforms were not worn, and the impression gained was of a caring environment, created in order to facilitate change. Sentences were indeterminate and the degree of 'demoralisation' of the young person was perhaps a more important factor in the meting out of such sentences and in terms of measuring progress made than the actual offences committed, which overwhelmingly tended to be of theft.   Resocialisation consisted of two major components: the completion of a basic education, and the gearing of an individual towards industrial production. Success rates, viewed from the point of reconviction were invariably put at seventy per cent, a figure gained from central sources.

Perhaps one House of Correction, Trzemeszno, stood out, for it was, we learned, the only secure House of Correction in Poland;   a small secure 'prison', very similar to English Victorian monoliths.

Here offences which had been committed by inmates were usually of a more serious and violent nature, and success rates were said to be lower as a result of the 'negative selection' of inmate population, whose behaviour had not been influenced by less secure establishments and who exhibited high levels of demoralisation.   For the first time also, uniformed prison officers were seen.   These were not included in staff establishments, as they were discipline staff on loan from the prison service - the adult prison at Inowrocław - in order to provide the security element necessary for the regime. Clearly the uniformed staff seemed to be more reserved and aloof in their dealings with inmates, generally observing behaviour and ensuring that set tasks were performed.

In terms of security, inmates were located in cells in numbers of between two and four per cell, and it was observed that 'wings' or units could easily be secured, staff then withdrawing to a certain defined perimeter.   Thus the role of the uniformed staff appeared to be different from that of those professionals whom we had previously met.   Up to this point an impression of 'caring paternalism' had been given by professional staff, whose attitude was well summed up in a slogan observed at the correctional house at Szubin, which quite simply stated that 'there are only men, and fools'.

Juvenile crime and delinquency places the Polish regime in a somewhat ironic and ideologically embarrassing position. How can crime be acknowledged to exist within a system which tends to rely upon the total conformity of its members to the corporate whole, with individuality generally frowned upon? The extent of the concern felt can be best seen, I feel, in terms of the commitment and effort channelled into dealing with juveniles whom the state itself has a stake in resocialising for its own future good. Where such efforts fail in achieving the necessary resocialisation, what was an embarrassment becomes a threat to state and ideology as juveniles mature towards adulthood. At this point, attempts to resocialise become exercises in containment, and commitment to change becomes a demand for conformity: those who fail are received into penitential establishments.

Given the focus on establishments catering for those aged 13 - 21 years (though generally most inmates were found to be between the ages of 15 and 17 years) and the fact that an adult was deemed to be 25 years and over, we were interested in what provision was provided for those between the ages of 17 and 25 years. More particularly, what were the attitudes of prison staff towards them, and how did their organisation and resulting regime reflect a change in the attitude of the state towards them?

A visit to a penitentiary outside Włocławek, catering for this age group enabled one to observe the practical and physical realities of this change in attitude, as well as an insight into the Polish prison service. This experience was limited only by the fact that a visit to an adult establishment was not included on our itinerary, which might have provided a better understanding and more comprehensive, and possibly more accurate, comparison. Of particular interest to myself, working at the time as a probation officer within HMP Hull (then a dispersal prison within the English penal system), were possible comparisons between Polish prison staff and their English counterparts.

I was initially struck by the imposing wall of the penitentiary, not in terms of its height or thickness, but by its length and the watchtowers manned by armed guards in paramilitary uniform. During my visit, I was most of all affected by what appeared to be a greater paramilitary influence than that found within the English prison service, and it was this aspect that I chose to research in an attempt to provide a comparison between the two services. This comparison became less pronounced as time elapsed and the number of similarities between the two services appeared to grow.

There are dangers in making a direct comparison, given the cultural and political differences of the two societies. The subject of comparison has to be seen in context - history providing the greatest difference in terms of respective views towards militarism and attitudes towards imprisonment. Bearing this in mind then, I will attempt to outline the basic points of my comparison, centring upon the militaristic features of prison organisation.

The Shorter Oxford English Dictionary defines militarism as the spirit and tendencies of the professional soldier; prevalence of military sentiment and ideas among a people, tendency to regard the military efficiency as the paramount interest of the state. Militarism refers to the vast array of attitudes, sentiment and ceremonial practices through which the ideological belief in the superiority of everything military to explain everything civilian is cultivated and continually reaffirmed (Lang, 1972). In such a sense then it has little to do with military capability or operations, and in respect of a prison service must, I feel, involve an ideological belief in a value system which is imposed upon another group and re-affirmed by certain shared attitudes, sentiments and practice.

The notion of discipline would appear to be central to any prison service and the organisational expression of this is in a paramilitary structure, whose justification is that prison staff are in a state of war, in a sense that action is rare and expectation of action is common (Thomas, 1980). An arena is military when the expectation of violence is high (Huntington). It is this expectation of crisis and conflict which then provides a parallel between the prison and military services.

The charges of any prison service are locked up against their will, thereby ensuring this conflict with its threat of violence within the setting of the prison. Several facets however, have to be seen as implicit if the prison staff, the organised minority, are to cope in the management of an ever increasing majority. Primarily, there has to be obedience which if control is to result, is more easily afforded within clearly. defined roles with individuals being aware of the boundaries of the power and functions. The English prison service was from the start a paramilitary organisation which quite naturally attracted those who could positively relate to an ethos reinforced by the wearing of uniform and its rank designed to inculcate a respect for authority (King and Morgan, 1980). In other nations too, the attraction was also mirrored with employment geared towards the ex-serviceman. Thus it was not only in England that large numbers were recruited.

At the first International Congress on the Prevention and Repression of Crime held in London in July 1872, several European courts reported that they preferred staff with military experience.   Prussia, Saxony, Wurttemberg tried to appoint ex-servicemen exclusively (Thomas, 1980).

Why did (and do) so many nations prefer ex-servicemen?   It is not merely because of their own personal and philosophical views concerning authority and its right to punish those who transgress the particular society's norms, but also because their former training and habits of order and discipline, of rendering and enforcing strict obedience and their aptitude in dealing with large bodies of men are valuable qualities, useful to the task at hand (Thomas, 1980).   If discipline is central to the development of prison services, then it has a corollary essential to the running of the prison, and that is order.

Within all societies, prisons are closed and secret institutions, to which most have no right of access.   It is usually a coercive regime, involving the enforced custody of society's law breakers: its staff too are constrained by such codes of discipline and a commitment to the goal of security, which are ever present within a secure penal establishment. For those in the prison service, alternative careers, certainly of a similar job security, will be hard to find, and with time, dependency upon the service will increase.

For the two camps within the prison setting, there can be no concensus of what behaviour would contribute to order, and where many are prepared to fight order, coercion will be necessary.   The resulting mistrust and fear of violent conflict, together with the need for security contributed towards the insularity of the staff who manifest a cohesion and esprit de corps similar to that of a military unit.   Because of a secrecy which pervades them, prison services are highly vulnerable to critical public opinion.   At such times, and especially when prison staff feel isolated from their own senior management, they are prone to become alienated from the very society that they serve, and this process which now seems characteristic of our prison staff, is actually endemic in modern prison systems (King and Morgan, 1980).

Thus prison services seem to have been organised along paramilitary lines, employing personnel who share a common ethos, to operate in penal establishments which share the task of containment and control.   Threat of conflict is high, the regime coercive, and the structure of the service thereby formed demands both discipline and order.   Staff cohesion is high, not only from the sharing of tasks, but also because of threats and fears generated both within and without the establishment.

The birth of the modern prison service in England came within the centralisation achieved by the Prisons Act of 1877. The prison administrators of those days had two major concerns. The first was that of contamination – the process of pushing the weak, inadequate or criminally unsophisticated, into conditions that exposed them to moral and physical danger. Two regimes, the silent and the separate, had developed as a means of dealing with this problem, and it was the latter that was to predominate. Through a policy of physical separation, association and communication, and thereby contamination, was checked. Separation had an even greater significance to staff: by controlling association and communication, they prevented prisoner collaboration and the development of hostile sub-cultures which, given the numerical superiority of prisoners, posed a threat to staff, control and security. Secondly, centralisation led to the concentration of power, formerly exercised locally, into the hands of the Home Secretary. The formation of a prison commission saw staff organised in a paramilitary structure with clearly defined authority and very definite sanctions if that authority was exceeded (Thomas, 1980).

The formal structure would hopefully result in better treatment of inmates and avoid those excesses previously witnessed prior to the Act in 1877. Whilst separation effectively came to an end in 1930, its legacy can be seen in the English prison system today in diluted form in the guise of regulated association, and the system of cellular confinement.

Separation in Poland was largely between classifications of inmates – first offenders, young prisoners, and recidivists, and there was little provision for separation within each major classification. Inmates occupied dormitories of varying size catering for six to twelve or more with security peripheral to the unit, just as the security of the prison as a whole seemed to be perimeter based. Within each dormitory unit, discipline was the responsibility of a nominated inmate, which in my view was an abrogation of the control necessary for the maintenance of safe and humane containment, and where the staff abrogate all control other than the perimeter, a highly complex society develops, characterised by great brutality (Thomas, 1972). Within the penitentiary, information concerning violent behaviour was contradictory; whilst we were informed that 80 per cent of inmates were violent and aggressive, not in terms of the crime committed, but in terms of behaviour within the establishment, it was also stated that acts of aggression within the establishment were few. It was further added that instances of homosexual rape were sent to court, where a maximum sentence of five years could be imposed, and that whilst criminal sub-cultures were a problem in 1980, there had since been a reduction in these phenomena.

My interpretation of this information was that a much lower percentage of violent acts was actually reported to staff than occurred. A major factor militating against the making of such reports is likely to be the dormitory system of confinement, where authority is delegated to individuals within each unit. Perhaps the delegation of such authority to certain individuals amongst the inmate group helps to cause a rift, a fracture within the sub-group, granting as it does to the privileged few a stake in the maintenance of the status quo. Given that such individuals are chosen to maintain discipline, it seems logical to assume that they are likely to be powerful characters in their own right, and such a process may consciously or otherwise, also sanction fear as a control mechanism. Or is the dormitory style, as Lammich says, the only practical possibility, in view of the chronic overcrowding of penal establishments in Poland; a means therefore of expediency. Given the continually rising prison population in England and its limited resources, this is a salutary thought.

As the use of fear might be deemed to be an inevitable consequence of a para-military structure, the perimeter based style of control also seems to lend itself to the military image as seen in the popular view of what constitutes a prisoner of war camp. This physical structure, together with the correlation between task and nature of the regime, is of importance. In some nineteenth century English convict prisons, work was performed by inmates under the control of a civil guard. They carried weapons, stood aloof from inmates performing work, and guarded the walls when inmates were in their cells. It was when inmates were working that their association and concentration posed greater threats to security, hence the different regime which reflected more closely the paramilitary ideal.

Reading such descriptions of 'public works' prisons mirrored closely my observations of the penitentiary visited, and the Polish system as a whole, in which labour is an obligation, privilege, and an essential element in achieving resocialisation. Indeed, since the beginning of the seventies, the practice of imprisonment has been mainly concentrated on strict formal discipline and the maximum exploitation of the work force of the prisoners - a practice that goes back to the early fifties (Rzeplinski, 1983).

Such a task then seems best achieved by a paramilitary service, equipped with arms to ensure the compliance of the sub-group with the work at hand, and in order to maintain the security necessary to control the movement of large groups of men engaged in tasks of labour. The 'shift' system of a large industrial concern also comes to mind and the dormitory system may also represent the most expedient means of marshalling and directing each 'shift' at any one point in time. Again, prison work is not regarded as laid down in the penal code, as being primarily educational, but that it is the economic factor which determines the type of work to which prisoners are assigned (Lammich, 1981).

Whilst the physical similarities between the penitentiary visited and the convict prisons of late nineteenth century England are quite striking, it would be foolhardy to suggest that this offered conclusive evidence of a stronger para-military influence in Poland today, although it may be regarded as a further indication that this may be the case. In drawing comparisons between the two, one thing certain is that in both the primary task is the containment and control of individuals sentenced to periods of incarceration for breaching a society's norms. Such a clarity of task also provides for a clarity of role that is found within the paramilitary model.

It is the wearing of uniform that visibly and readily distinguished the prison service as a paramilitary structure, emphasing a common purpose and role, whilst also emphasising the difference from those who do not wear the same uniform. Both services wear uniforms, yet it was the Polish service that seemingly mirrored more accurately the armed forces, having both a ceremonial and a 'battle' dress, further strengthened by the fact that arms are carried in the performance of their task. Article 2.1 of the Act of 10 December 1959 (including the amendment of 12 June 1975) states that the prison service is a uniform formation equipped with arms (Rzeplinski, 1983).

Leaving aside the carrying of such arms, the wearing of a uniform itself emphasises disparity, and in the prison setting where high status is not readily conceded to a personality, especially by prisoners, the uniform is a valuable role sign, ascribing status, high in the case of staff, low in the case of prisoners, to the people wearing it (Thomas, 1972). This is particularly true of the Polish service, where all staff wear uniform, in comparison to the English service, where arguably the greatest status accrues to governor grades who do not (as yet) wear uniform. However, within both services the differences between the officer and inmate groups are highlighted by the wearing of uniform and by a discipline within which rank is designed to inculcate respect for authority (Thomas, 1972) and as promotion is gained, uniform and rank are identifiably different.

Yet does the carrying of arms and the presence of a much more military recognisable uniform necessarily mean that the Polish service is much more militaristic than the English? Surely elements of its structure and methods of operation and regime prove to be more accurate indices than the outward embodiment; and in looking at such aspects of the two services, a comparison can hopefully be achieved.

The paramilitary structure is seen by many as a crisis controlling structure and as such suitable to a prison with control as a primary task. It provides for management, or command, almost exclusively from the top downwards. Roles are clearly defined and the parameters of one's brief are clearly laid down also, thus limiting the degree of discretion exercised. To work within such well defined parameters means therefore, that all men within that grade are interchangeable. As stated, there is a premium on the downward flow of information and orders, which staff lower down on the hierarchy are expected to obey, the rationale being that in the event of a crisis, there is little time to discuss matters; decisions have to be made and translated into action quickly. The military authority structure is geared to one overriding requirement: the uniform directions of troops in battle. The ability to reach quick decisions under external pressure is critical. Hierarchy rather than equality provides the basis for unity (Lang, 1972).

Such a rigid pattern of communication is most acceptable where the amount of time in service is linked to expertise and the ability to function effectively is enhanced by the accumulation of experience. However, whilst the monopoly of information provides staff with a legitimacy and whilst orders flow smoothly downwards, there is almost an obsession to hold information back at almost every rank unless its dissemination has the clear approval of superiors. Also dysfunctioning can result when such individuals are reluctant to act or to accept responsibility at times of crisis, preferring to leave decision-making to superiors.

Within such an atmosphere, rumour and speculation, uncertainty and mistrust develop, particularly as those lower down the chain have to pass upwards information gained as quickly as possible. There is little room for discussion, hence orders and instructions are generally clear and comprehensible. The structure also allows for the supervision of staff, not as in the nurturing of an individual's development, but in the administration of sanctions, should rules or orders be broken or disobeyed. Whilst both services developed out of the paramilitary model, it is the Polish service that remains closer to the ideal, which can be seen in points of contrast, arising out of the reformative developments that have affected the English service.

It was the Gladstone Commission Report of 1895 that heralded the beginning of the move away from the paramilitary model, and entry into an era of confusion and doubt. The report introduced the principle that besides the primary task of containment and control, there should also be a concurrent task of reformation. Thus containment and control, tasks which were achieved so well through a rigid hierarchical structure, were no longer to be the sole tasks of the English prison service. Yet the task of reformation clearly calls for a different structure if logically, decisions are to be made on the requirement of each individual. In doing so, case discussions and airing of grievances would be allowed and in dealing with the individual inmate the prison officer would be allowed a degree of discretion. Orders would be questioned, not immediately obeyed, and perhaps even modified prior to implementation.

To place reformatory ideals as a primary task, upon a structure best suited to the maintenance of discipline and order, containment and control constrained by an individual's subscription to an ethos far removed from reformatory aims, could only result in confusion, uncertainty and alienation of the officer groups. As reformative policies developed, so did conflicts between the custodial and reformative aims. The practical changes that were to occur over the next sixty years or so were to impinge upon the purity of the paramilitary model and it is these aspects above all that provide a contrast with the Polish service.

The Gladstone Report put forward the view that the governor should be brought into closer personal contact with inmates, with charismatic governors positively influencing the inmate population. Appointments were subsequently made on this basis, with little attention paid to the administrative qualities of appointees. The decision was to have an even greater effect upon the views of prison staff, who, increasingly, saw the governor as being there largely to side with the prisoners. They felt that new reformative measures would make their task more difficult; as separation decreased, association increased and incentives were introduced as a means of maintaining greater control. Such incentives were to mean little to the ever increasing group of long term inmates following the abolition of capital punishment, when the task of control became even more difficult. In the succeeding sixty years these developments were to make up an overall change in the operation of the prison service, which was to create a profound sense of alienation on the part of the officers.

Within the English system, governors constitute the line management concerned with the primary task of ensuring safe custody and the governor is still an influential person, having the ability to shape the nature of a prison, able to demonstrate what is acceptable and what is not. However, a problematic feature in respect to the governor grade is the promotional structure which leads to frequent movement, and consequent uncertainty about whether plans and regime introduced by governors will be either further developed or abandoned; a process which hardly encourages or sustains the strength and morale of the service. The introduction of lower tiers of the governor grade, the assistant governor, further disturbed the command structure; a process further extended by the introduction into the system of other specialists from outside, with little in common with and little understanding of the rigidity of the traditional command structure of uniformed staff. Indeed, the officer group considered such individuals more likely to sympathise with the inmates than with themselves. In the years of reform, they believed the division between the prisoners and the specialists, including the governors, was narrowing and the gap betwene the latter and the officers was widening (Thomas and Pooley, 1980).

The assistant governor occupies an ambiguous position in the prison service, a position clearly reflected upon in the post mortem that followed the Hull prison riot of 1976, when it was openly acknowledged that confusion existed as to whom the uniformed staff, including principal and senior officers were responsible, the chief officer or the assistant governor. Changes have occurred since that riot, but, in my view, the problem persists as can be seen in the rivalry that exists between many wing principal officers and wing assistant governors.

The introduction of specialists, teachers, psychologists, probation officers, at times of increasing financial restraint also led to feelings amongst staff that what limited resources were available were being pumped into the inmate sector rather than their own. The introduction of specialism further complicated the organisational structure of the service; besides the line staff who carried out specialist tasks (hospital officers, caterers, PEI's, instructors, works officers, etc.) other professionals had established a presence within the service including the medical officer, chaplain, educational staff, probation staff, psychologists, industrial managers, administrative staff and other civil servants. These specialists were a real threat to the position of uniformed staff, having views about administration, their place within the organisation and more significantly, had different perspectives about organisational goals, and were prepared to assert their own demands for prestige and influence.

Such an organisational structure greatly complicates the traditional paramilitary command structure. Whilst the relationship of professional staff to uniformed staff is not harmonious, a great deal of the success of an institution in its rehabilitative efforts necessarily depends upon the degree to which the professional staff are accepted, not only by the prisoners, but by each other and by other members of the prison staff (Hall Williams, 1970). Differences in policy and practice abound. Policy is that broad framework within which a prison service operates: practice the translation of that policy into the daily routine of the system. The introduction of the parole system was a policy highly subject to staff influence in its operation, particularly through reports based on inmates' attitudes and behaviour towards staff. At the end of the day, it is the officers who decide not only whether they themselves will be involved, but whether anyone else will be allowed to maximise his effort (Thomas, 1977).

Prisoners can always fail to be produced, lists mislaid, professionals delayed, and receipt of orders denied. Despite the changes that have taken place within the prison system, the officer group have, I feel, largely been able to maintain their cohesion and identity and further have successfully prevented the ascendence of any of the other groups within the prison setting. This is particularly true of the prison service in Poland, where there is a very clear paramilitary structure. The position of an officer within the service is defined — since 1975 — by military rank and the head of the prison service has the rank of general (Rzeplinski, 1983).

In England the prison service comes under the direct authority of the Home Secretary. In Poland it is organised as a similarly autonomous part of the administrative system of the Minister of Justice. Whilst the English director-general is an under secretary of state in the Home Office, in Poland the general-director, directly responsible to the Minister, has the military rank of general and is the effective head of the prison service, able to shape penitentiary policy throughout Poland and does so by inventing internal regulations called 'the guiding rules' (Rzeplinski, 1983). These are not necessarily within the Act of 10 December 1959 and legal regulations are changed according to situation. This Act does not leave any room for doubts: Article 1 states that the prison service is created to perform the tasks concerning execution of the deprivation of liberty and of detention (Rzeplinski, 1983). Article 20.1 states that its personnel are obliged to serve faithfully the people's Poland, to guard the people's democracy and law, order and public security.

Such regulations define the work of the prison officers and clearly oblige them to treat prisoners in a very strict and formal way. Thus the important task of the prison service in Poland is the execution of the punishment and not the educational or other rehabilitative task. The task is clear, and the structure reflects a purity towards the ideal model that the English prison service lost in essence with the report of 1895. The confusion is even seen in the rules that officers have to operate. Prison rule 1 states that the purpose of training and treatment shall be to encourage a good and useful life. Yet the committal that accompanies the newly sentenced prisoner leaves no such doubt, stating that containment is the task to be fulfilled. In the Polish system, Article 20.1 (above) would seem to infer the swearing of an allegiance similar to oaths sworn upon joining the armed forces, yet in England too the newly entrant prison officer signs the official secrets act and swears to honour and obey the Queen and State, and similarly to obey all orders. However, whilst the Polish prison officer clearly relates to prisoners in a very strict and formal way, in England the very system determines this relationship.

Staff working with the dispersal system are encouraged to talk to inmates, the regime requiring communication and relationships; the training prisons are organised along similar lines, though to a lesser degree. The local prison does less to encourage informal communication with inmates, being much more structured in order to cope with a widely fluctuating population. The English prison rules are legal instruments open to judicial interpretation and whilst standing orders are not regulated by law, circular instructions are. Such regulations are not as easily changed as they may be in Poland in order to accommodate administrative needs.

The Polish central administration is divided into eight district boards, organised along lines similar to HPDI. As its boundaries do not follow administrative areas, they are not under the control of local administration. In this respect the structure is similar to those in England.

At establishment level each institution in Poland is firmly governed by one person, the warden or governor, clearly identified by military rank and accorded the respect that such a rank deserves through the deferential treatment paid by subordinates. The colonel who hosted our visit was treated in this way by his staff.

Unlike a governor within the English system whose power has been eroded with time, the warden has a much more total, almost autocratic role, being responsible for all decisions concerning the organisation of work within the prison, punishing or rewarding prisoners and shaping the conditions of a prisoner's isolation. He is head of the whole administrative system of the institution, consisting of the following departments: security, penitentiary, classification, employment, economic, financial and in some bigger prisons, health service (Rzeplinski, 1983).

As a result the deference accorded the governor is much more pronounced than in England in relation to a 'civilian' governor, even though prison officer staff remain respectful in the paramilitary sense. Such respect from the uniform staff, is reinforced by the close working, as well as hierarchical, relationship between the governor and the uniformed chief prison officer.

The English governor's power is nonetheless limited. He is restricted in relation to the promotion of staff, and there is no power to transfer or even dismiss staff: thus whilst held accountable for an institution, the governors have little control over resources.

Even visiting inspectors and assistant regional directors are often unable to readily effect change, and there exists the feeling amongst staff that it is civil servants at the Home Office, far removed from the realities of the situation, and who have perhaps never even been inside a prison, who hold the power. Clearly then, the line of command, whilst visible (despite the greater organisational complexities) has a limited impact, hedged about as it is by administrative factors and bureaucratic delay.

The prison disturbances of 1972 led to the 'low key' response from the Home Office when uniformed staff clearly felt that action was required by a service traditionally organised to provide a positive stance. This is one of the reasons behind the actions of staff in recent years, who discovered that inaction created a power vacuum that could easily be filled. This was the beginning of a process which has become hardened into an everyday tactic of many prison staff. It is to take unilateral action, to refuse to obey orders, and to withold labour, so as to put the burden for resolving the consequent disorder upon the prison epartment (Thomas and Pooley, 1980). Sadly it seems that it is again the governor who has to cope with such militancy and deal with officers who, as a result of central confusion over aims and tasks and the means of achieving them have moved from paramilitary discipline to anarchy (King and Morgan, 1980).

In Poland the purity of the structure of the prison service

in paramilitary terms has produced a hierarchical system run on military lines, and this defines the internal relationships between individuals of higher and lower ranks. The warden pays attention to the requirements and expectations of those people and groups whom he considers to be the source of his power. In such a situation, the main grade prison staff can work without giving too much thought to the needs of prisoners. The essence of their work lies in fulfilling the arbitrarily defined needs of society and the requirements of supervision (Rzeplinski, 1983).

It is the penitentiary commission of the institution which has the task concerning the welfare of inmates – yet it is called into existence by the warden who does not have to listen to its opinions. Whilst the minister in the 1970s had little power in influencing personnel, prison, or prison rules, he did control the system of penitentiary judges, who had unlimited right of judicial control concerning inmates. Their activities, says Rzeplinski, were inconvenient for staff. The judges looked closely at any complaints that affected the basic rights of the prisoner, a policy that was fiercely criticised by prison staff who felt the judges were siding with the inmates and not with them. Since this time the power or position of the judge has become rather formal and prison staff limit actual contact with inmates. As a result the visits made by such judges appear to have become rarer.

In spite of the lack of formal links with the Ministry of the Interior, many personnel of the public security systems were obtaining posts in penitentiary establishments and there is increasing contact between the police and prison security staff. There are few 'outsiders' within the structure and rehabilitative work is carried out by prison officials: uniformed pedagogues, psychologists and sociologists. They are also linked to the paramilitary structure and are armed which introduces an 'irrational element' in their relationships with both staff and inmates. Even the prison doctor can be a member of the prison service, though this is dependent upon the type of institution.

Even in Poland, however, the prison staff experienced a degree of alienation in the 1970s and early 1980s with a 'feeling of pauperisation as compared with the militia and the army'. The development of the trades union movement in the autumn of 1980 also showed them the lack of any real protection of ordinary prison staff against the arbitrary and frequently changing decisions of their superiors: wardens making their own 'private penitentiary policy'.

December 1980 saw a national meeting of prison staff in an

attempt to counteract growing dissatisfaction, yet at a time of 'union' feeling, no trade union appeared. 1981 saw a riot at Kaminsk following which prison staff delegates met with a commission from the Ministry of Justice and demanded amongst other items, protection against prisoners and an abandonment of liberal changes in prison regimes introduced on 19 May 1981. Staff felt uneasy as a result of proved complaints against them by prisoners. These experiences led the staff, with their very strong paramilitary structure and lines of communication, to resist any chagnes of a reformative or liberal nature.

Such control is also maintained by the power to grant privileges and to invoke disciplinary measures: such privileges include the granting of permission to receive food parcels, to extend visiting periods and to allow greater frequency of correspondence. Disciplinary measures can be imposed by the governor, the most severe of which are laid down in the penal code of 1969, including withdrawal of visiting rights for up to three months and solitary confinement for up to fourteen days. Other measures include the curtailment of private correspondence for up to three months, a reduction in rations in cases of refusing to work, and confinement in an isolation cell for up to one month. This entails confinement in conditions rendering contact with other prisoners impossible, no visits are allowed, and no letters are allowed to be sent or received.

Thus disciplinary measures are direct and punitive, the prisoner has no right of appeal against disciplinary measures (Lammich, 1981). The paramilitary structure itself sets the standards and metes out the punishments. In the English system the more severe punishments can only be awarded by the board of visitors, lay magistrates from outside the prison service, whose decisions are now subject to judicial review.

Thus at this point in time, despite the many similarities, the Polish prison service appears more 'pure' in terms of its proximity to the model ideal of a paramilitary structure, than to the prison service in England. It therefore follows that it is a more paramilitary style body than the English, having well defined aims, and a clear role to perform. Its structure is hierarchical without the many 'professional' complications that detract in England from the simple hierarchical communication and command network. However, since the Mountbatten Report, there has been a gradual shift in the English service, and there exists a desire to move even further towards the model ideal.

Mountbatten, despite recommending that there should be an increase in the number of prison probation officers, primarily gave the prison service a definite and straightforward task that could best utilise the basic paramilitary structure — namely the task of humane confinement. Whilst many inconsistencies remain, there has in my view been a subtle, yet of late, accelerating trend to revert to a structure more reminiscent of that introduced in the nineteenth century.

The displacement of the borstal system by a system of youth custody has emphasised again the demand for containment, security and control. This is illustrated by the fact that officers who used to wear civilian clothes in the borstals now all wear uniform. What then will be the next step? There is much talk about a return to 'black traditional' uniforms. There is also great interest in the mangement structure review of 1985, which is expected to put forward its findings in 1986. Informed speculation and expectation is that all staff — including governor grades, the administrative officer and other civil servants — will return to uniform. If that transpires it would be the most significant move in recent years.

In summary, I have suggested areas of comparison that do show the Polish prison service to be a more paramilitary body than the English prison service. This is primarily because of the reformative aims of the English service deriving from the Gladstone Report of 1895, which seriously disputed the paramilitary ethos. It would appear that future development may see the English service moving closer to the position currently enjoyed by the Polish prison service.

6 Deviancy, disorder and social control in Poland and England in the early 1980s

JILL CARPENTER

Abstract

Having first briefly described the social and political scenes
in the early 1980s in Poland and England, I plan to locate
these differing events and responses within an understanding of
the sociology of deviance and social control and to illustrate
some of these similarities.   In Poland, there were widespread
strikes, leading to the formation of the 'free trade union'
Solidarity and to various developments and reforms, but the
period culminated in December 1981 with the imposition of
martial law.   The disorders in England were more sporadic and
of a different nature, including the urban riots of 1981 and
1985, and the miners strike of 1984 - 1985.   However, when we
begin to look at these examples of disorder from a sociological
point of view, many similarities begin to be apparent.
Equally, there are parallels to be drawn between the official
responses of the two governments and the institutions they
control.   I will then show how the official responses
reflected societal and governmental stances on deviancy and law
and order in general, within which, there are, I will argue,
more similarities than might immediately be apparent.
Finally, I aim to look at some of the reasons why these popular
movements of dissent ultimately failed, again trying to draw
parallels between the two situations.

* * * * *

Deviance can be described as banned or controlled behaviour which is likely to attract punishment or disapproval, in other words it is primarily, though not necessarily, exclusively illegal behaviour which is likely to be met by the appropriate methods of social control. Social control in its turn can be defined as the organised ways in which society responds to behaviour and people it regards as deviant, problematic, worrying, threatening, troublesome, or undesireable in some way or other. The term is sometimes used to include all social processes designed to induce conformity or as a negative term to cover not just the obviously coercive apparatus of the state but also the punative hidden element in all state sponsored social policy. The term social control can be used to include the repression of political opposition but is more ordinarily confined to the organised response to crime, delinquency and allied forms of deviant and/or socially problematic behaviour.

Using these definitions can the events in Poland in 1980 - 1981, the disorders in England in 1981 and 1985, and the miners' strike and the official responses to them be described as deviancy and examples of social control? I would argue that they can, although the political nature of all the events tends to cloud the issue. Looked at from the authorities' point of view, both the strikes in Poland and the disorders in England were problematic, involving, in different degrees, illegal behaviour (in Poland the tearing up of railway lines on one occasion; in the 1981 riots acts of arson, theft and assaults on police and in the miners' strike behaviour likely to cause a breach of the peace). These events were certainly deviant in that they differed from the norm - although in both countries not dissimilar events can be traced back through the history of working class dissent.

The events had at their roots economic factors, particularly the notion of comparative deprivation. The Polish workers had enjoyed increases in their standards of living, but saw this as under threat. The same could be said of the miners whose wages were comparatively high, but stood to lose all hope of future employment through pit closures. In the case of inner city youth, their deprivations were in many ways absolute - no jobs, poor housing, poor education - but their poverty was particularly acute against a background of conspicious consumerism.

But taking a sociological perspective can other parallels be drawn in explaining these different events? There were two sociological approaches for explaining the riots, a functionalist approach and a conflictual model (Taylor, 1983). Functionalism sees society as a set of individuals and groups held together by a moral consensus. Under this approach, crime is normal - an integral part of all healthy societies serving to heighten collective sentiments, sharpen perceptions of moral imperatives, more tightly integrate society against the transgressor (Downes and Rock, 1982). Thus a certain amount of deviance is functional but too much is pathological and the riots (and the violence on picket lines in the miners' strike) were a consequence of a malfunction of the social system which was unable to adapt to a new situation (the decline of the inner cities, the breakdown in police community relations, the situation on the picket lines). There thus developed in both the inner cities and the mining communities a potential for collective violence which became actual violence when a precipitating factor, for example 'Swamp 81' in Brixton, put the discontent into a specific and reinforcing context leading to a build up of fear and antagonism which was eventually expressed in violence.

Alternatively, if one adopts a conflictual model of society, the riots and the miners' strike can both be seen as examples of subservient groups, attempting to rise against the dominant group. Depending on one's stance within this framework, the riots can either be seen as the early conflicts by which a nascent proletariat begins to lash out against capitalist exploitation, or, dividing society into racial groups instead, as instances of protest by exploited races, which herald racial revolution, or yet again by dividing society into groups with competing interests rather than structurally defined groups, as the protests of consistent losers anxious to obtain some redistribution of resources in their favour.

Taylor also describes two socio-psychological approaches which could be used to explain the riots, or at least individuals' involvement in them. Firstly, there is the notion of cognitive dissonance which explains why, when the performance of an economic, political or social system falls short on individual's expectations, he experiences tension and is motivated towards behaviour which might include rioting or picket line violence, designed to alleviate dissonance or bring together the expectations and the real situation. The other approach mentioned is the frustration-aggression model. Using this model, individuals, who are prevented from achieving their goals, become frustrated; sustained frustration leads to psychological tension which is automatically transferred into aggression and thence to violence. The common element in both approaches is the notice of individuals acting non-rationally, spurred towards violence by unconscious and uncontrollable mental processes. Thus, while the frustration-aggression model might explain why some individual miners (or police officers) indulged in uncharacteristic violence on the picket line, it does nothing to explain the build up of tension in the inner cities or the miners' decision to strike.

Can any of these approaches helpfully be applied to the situation in Poland in 1980 - 1981? To start with the first of the strictly sociological approaches, namely functionalism - can the actions of the workers and the formation of Solidarity be described as a result of a malfunction of the social system in Poland. Clearly, within the Polish social system such behaviour would normally be viewed as deviant but perhaps 'functional'. Early disturbances on a much smaller scale had been dealt with harshly but also not infrequently resulted in reforms which although often short lived seemed to reinforce the existing social and political systems. In 1980 - 1981 the protests met with such widespread support that the very survival of the existing system appeared under threat. Slowly, however, the population as a whole, encouraged by the regime, began to distance itself at least from the radical activists in Solidarity. The regime imposed martial law in the belief that this would be acceptable to the majority as an alternative to the perceived threatened overthrow of the government. Their perceptions, however, were inaccurate and martial law was not welcomed, but greeted largely by apathy and resignation. Thus, in the long run perhaps the way Solidarity developed was 'functional' in that it allowed the regime to regain control without undue protest. The population's wish for stability and fear of outside intervention were, in the end, paramount. The radical wing of Solidarity became the 'transgressor' against which the rest of society needed to protect itself, thereby resigning itself to the controls placed upon it by the regime.

Adopting a conflictual model of society, clearly the approach dividing society into racial groups cannot apply to Poland, but can either of the other models be transferred to a system which, after all, is 'socialist'? Clearly the workers did see themselves as having different interests from the authorities and can therefore perhaps be seen as consistent losers who were anxious to obtain some redistribution of resources - financial and regarding political influence. Despite increases in standards of living there were still vast differences between the life styles of ordinary workers and those in privileged positions and also in terms of political power. Indeed it could also be argued that the workers' protests were an example of the proletariat attempting, with some, but not lasting, success, to rise against capitalism - in this case state capitalism. They suggest that the attempt was unsuccessful, partly because the workers did not see themselves in this light; they wanted increased freedom and influence but could not see that this was impossible without overthrowing the regime. By the time they began to realise this, it was too late, the regime had regained the initiative and was able to impose martial law, thereby leaving the apparatus of state capitalism largely unfettered, in the end, by workers control (Barker & Weber, 1982).

Moving on to the psycho-sociological approaches detailed earlier, I intend only to consider the notion of cognitive dissonance as the frustration-aggression model would not seem to apply to the Polish workers' protests where violence was largely avoided. Certainly, the workers might have been described as suffering cognitive dissonance in the late 1970s as their expectations of increased living standards were not met; this did appear to result in a build up of tension, demonstrated by surveys which showed increased dissatisfaction and frustration against those in privileged positions. The workers did respond by behaviours designed to bring their situations more closely into line with their expectations, thus, arguably, reducing dissonance. However, I would suggest that their actions were much more consciously motivated than the notion of cognitive dissonance allows.

I now progress to consider the varying official responses to the events in question, and how these illustrate the concepts of social control in the two countries. In both cases, the responses were complex, including both conciliatory and repressive measures and both had the result (eventually in the Polish situation, more immediately in England) of marginalising the deviants and thereby maintaining the status quo. In England, the governmental response to the 1981 disorders was two-fold: firstly the disorders themselves were quelled by police action, gradually regaining control of the riot torn area and arresting numbers of participants; the disorders wree then portrayed as largely criminal actions and the participants punished by means of the criminal justice system (court and custody). Secondly, a conciliatory response was followed, initially by setting up of the Scarman inquiry empowered to look into the larger social reasons for the disorders as well as the riots themselves. However, his recommendations were not followed in any more than a cosmetic or piecemeal fashion. As mentioned earlier, some reforms took place with the police, but their powers were also increased, and very little real action has been taken to improve the problems of the inner cities – certainly not sufficient to prevent further disorders in 1985. The governmental response to the miners' strike was more straightforward and falls readily into the boundaries of what we understand by social control. Goodman shows that there is plently of evidence to suggest that the government planned in advance: no one can now seriously dispute that the government was determined to ensnare Arthur Scargill and the NUM into a trap, and then proceeded to use the police, who became the crucial arm of government during the dispute to break the strike (Mason, 1985). Indeed there were many significant and some would say dangerous developments of police and court powers at the time of the strike, including the use of the national reporting centre, constituting the virtual setting up of a national police force, using roadblocks to stop potential pickets entering certain counties, or even on one occasion travelling north of the River Thames, large scale, militarised police presence on picket lines, the setting up of special courts to handle the massive influx of pickets and a new selective use of the Bail Act, the standard bail condition for any picket arrested for obstructing the police was that the defendant should not go to any NCB property other than their place of work (Goodman, 1974). Thus, the strikers were subjected to the full wieght of the state social control systems involving in some instances imprisonment.

In Poland the regime's response was at first very different, consisting primarily of negotiation in the early stages and progressing to a reformist response as Solidarity developed into a broader social movement and thus a more influential, negotiating partner. In the long run, however, social control was re-imposed by repressive means, particularly by the use of the military and imprisonment. In December 1981 in response to what the regime interpreted as a threatened take over, martial law was imposed and when repression came it was in extreme form. Thousands of Solidarity leaders and workers were arrested and interned. Militant workers in the plants which resisted were arrested and gaoled in summary trials. Silesian miners and others were shot and beaten to death, others were severely beaten. Tanks and armoured cars patrolled the streets. The telephone network was shut down; travel on public transport tightly controlled. The armed forces took over press and TV and jammed foreign broadcasts. The borders were closed. Solidarity continued to function as an underground movement but any demonstrations of popular support were crushed. For example, on 3 May 1982 in Warsaw there was a demonstration of support for Solidarity but 'the Zomo' (motorised riot police) reacted with force, dispersing the crowd with water cannon, tear gas and truncheons. Thousands of protestors were arrested.

Thus, in both countries the governmental response to the events demonstrated a determination to maintain or re-impose control, utilising the usual organised responses to crime and delinquency, namely police, courts, imprisonment and, in Poland, the military. Whether we interpret social control as meaning the repression of political opposition or the ways in which society responds to deviant behaviour, we can still say that social control was imposed in response to the events, for the means adopted were those normally utilised against deviancy and delinquency, but, at the same time, it is clear that in both countries the events were interpreted as a political threat which needed to be repressed, whether this perception was accurate in any of the cases is another matter and open to question. Thus, it would seem that these means were adopted by the governments in both cases partly at least because the events were seen as a threat. However, the same social control devices are also used in other situations in response to crime and delinquency in the more usually accepted understanding of the terms. What light do the official responses to these events throw upon the wider issues of law and order in the two settings?

In England, the law and order issue increasingly dominates both political and popular thinking. Statistics suggest an ever increasing crime rate; the reporting of crime dominates the popular press. Despite significant developments in the area of 'community alternatives' the prison population continues to rise. We frequently read of new developments such as reparation schemes and neighbourhood watch. Police numbers have been increased as have police powers, with the new Police and Criminal Evidence Act. All this keeps the issue very much to the fore. It is also now generally accepted that official responses, the means of social control, have both hardened, thus the increased numbers of young people receiving custodial sentences, and broadened, reaching out to include deviants who would not have previously entered the control/welfare nets. At the same time, there has been a move away from the treatment model to the judicial model, a view that deviants should be punished rather than helped.

In Poland, from my observations on the exchange, and from discussions with our Polish colleagues, the opposite would appear to be the case. Andrzej Mosciskier's paper suggests that there is not a worrying rise in delinquency in Poland [Mosciskier, 1985) while other papers discussed revealed a trend towards a treatment model. Particularly indicative of this approach were the institutions for young people visited on the exchange, both of which demonstrated intensive input in the areas of employment and education and the promotion of supportive staff-inmate relationships. However, there did appear to be a point at which this level of intervention ceased, apparently around the age of 25. After this age, if criminality continues, it would appear to be dealt with more punitively, and prisons for these offenders appear to be run on much more militaristic lines.

The situation in England can therefore be described, in admittedly simplistic terms, as increasingly interventionist, hard line and punitive, reflecting an apparently high level of continuing concern about crime. The government's response to the 1981 and 1985 disorders and the miners' strike followed similar lines. A certain viewpoint of the events was encouraged, thus the press accusations of the involvement of political agitators in the disorders and the depiction of Scargil as wanting to topple the government. The full weight of the criminal justice system was brought to bear upon the participants and little attention was given to the underlying reasons for the alienation that fuelled the disorders.

On the other hand, the regime's attitudes to delinquency in Poland are more treatment orientated, at least, until a certain point in the criminal career of a young person. After this point, heavily repressive methods are utilised. Similarly, in response to the manifestations of deviancy experienced as a result of the formation of Solidarity, the attitude was initially conciliatory, but, later extremely repressive. Possibly, this reflects the difficulties that a regime in a socialist state experiences in acknowledging the reality of working class opposition, or, for that matter, crime, or anything other than an individual pathology based level. For if the state truly represents the people, how can the populace rise against it? And, if the people have a share in the regime, why do they feel the need to steal, if not for pathological and therefore treatable reasons? In any event, it is possible to draw parallels between the regime's responses to the events we have considered, and their social control policies as a whole.

This leads on to the question of similarities between the two regimes' social control and welfare policies. The usual stereotype of the Eastern European social system is of strict control in relation to a 'freer' system in the West. Yet, from what we have seen both in relation to the events we have considered and the social control policies, the reverse would appear to be the case. The Polish criminal justice system is indeed highly interventionist, but then so is the English system, and increasingly so. The Polish system though treatment orientated, still emphasises employment and good citizenship, but so too does the English system, for example in the probation order condition to 'lead an industrious life'. The Polish system is open about its motives, employing the term 'resocialisation' to the rehabilitative process, while the English system adopts more subtle means and language towards a very similar end. I would therefore suggest that the greater freedoms enjoyed by the west are illusory, at least for those individuals embroiled in the criminal justice system. And, as we have seen by an examination of the 1981 and 1985 disorders and the miners' strike, this includes an increasing number of people who clash with the system because of the political views, or who are alienated from the system because of political decisions.

There is one other important similarity between the English and Polish situations. I refer to the fact that in both cases the protests we have examined ultimately failed. The disorders of 1981 may have to be the first attempts of a deprived proletariat to lash out at capitalism: the miners' strike may have had its revolutionary aspects and Solidarity may have represented workers' interests against state capitalism, but all were doomed to failure, for the same reason, namely that piecemeal protests, like piecemeal reforms, cannot ultimately change the situation. In the case of the riots, political issues clearly do underlie the levels of deprivation and alienation that fuelled the participants' anger, but the outbursts were far from revolutionary. The miners' strike on the other hand was viewed by the government as a major political challenge and a threat to democratic rule which had to be put down, but it was far more of an emotional explosion of anger, wrath and frustration than a carefully planned political attack on the Thatcher government (Goodman, 1974). The Polish workers' movement, revolution, might have been possible but for the fact that there was no revolutionary socialist organisation in Poland and that therefore no systematic attempt has been made to spread the word that the workers should take power for themselves (Barker and Weber, 1982). Thus the governments were able to marginalise the rioters, the striking miners and protesting workers, to make them into deviants against which society would wish to protect itself by imposing social control and using all the weapons of the state against 'the enemy within' as the miners were described. However, in both the case of the miners and the Polish workers, the regimes over reacted, imposing stronger controls than the population found acceptable, thus perhaps sowing the seeds for further protest movements in the future.

In many ways, therefore, the social, political and welfare/ control systems in the two countries are not so very different as a superficial view of them would suggest. Perhaps the most enlightening lesson that can be learned from such comparisons and from an experience such as the Polish exchange, is that the freedoms upon which we pride ourselves in the west are not so great and that the controls upon the individual's freedom are more extensive than we imagine.

Conclusion

BRENDA PALMER

This second exchange with Poland followed the pattern
established in 1979 of co-operation between the Polish Ministry
of Justice, the University of Warsaw Institute of
Resocialisation, the North East London Polytechnic and the
South East Regional Staff Development Unit of the Probation
Service. The link between the two countries has felt to be
very strong since the earlier exchange in 1979. There have
been regular visits between NELP and the Institute for study
and between the organisers for purposes of delivering papers,
teaching and exploring further exchange possibilities.

Some of the members of the Polish group in 1984 were
academics, whose subjects were sociology, criminology and
psychology. There were two senior managers from the Ministry
of Justice, one of whom was responsible for a region
surrounding Posnan, and who was directly responsible for
probation practitioners in that area, the other being the
director of a House of Correction for girls aged 13 to 21.
Other members were practitioners both in the probation service
and in related practice such as family diagnostic centres, and
a journalist from the Ministry of Justice. The last was
specially interested in visiting different facilities in
England, and wrote about these for the ministry's journal,
which is distributed throughout the organisation.

The first part of the exchange, in September 1984, was held

in Britain.   The visiting Polish group were paired with probation officers representing practitioner and management grades from probation services throughout England, with whom the Polish members stayed for one of the two weeks of this part of the course.

The programme was divided into three sections.   In the first the whole group were in a conference centre in Essex, where members of the English group presented an overview of the criminal justice system to their Polish colleagues, to provide a basis of information which could be developed during the second section of the exchange.   At this point it was felt that too detailed an examination of the legal system, the courts and the welfare system could be confusing.   Instead each English member presented an aspect of their work, which was felt to be representative of the probation service's work within the community, the courts and in relation to after care.

It was important that the method of presentation varied and that the material was clearly explained.   A variety of methods were used, including case presentations, exercises which involved members making judgments about what they felt might happen in relation to the court setting, and talks using video, visual display and role play.   In this way it was hoped that the Polish visitors would have enough basic information to start their exploration into the English system when they were visiting their partners in their work settings.

The second section, which lasted a week, is a crucial part of this kind of exchange.   Each English and Polish pair returned to the home of the English partner, and lived and worked together for a week.   The intention is to allow the visitor an opportunity to experience a week in the working life of their partner, as well as to become part of their partner's home life.   Wherever possible, there has previously been correspondence between the partners, and often the visitor has given some indications of the areas of interest or particular aspects of the English system he or she wishes to see.   If the English partner does not visit and does not have information available about the particular concerns of their visitor, they will make arrangements for the Polish partner to make special visits.   The programme is therefore based upon the English partner's particular job, and the visiting partner's particular interests.   Where possible, the English are encouraged not to provide a specialised programme of visits, but rather to follow as normal a working week as possible so that their partners can develop an understanding of the demands placed upon workers in their position in England.   It was interesting for both groups to experience working with a partner whose job was often very dissimilar, though within the same field, and it was valuable to learn about the varying demands of the criminal justice system.

The third and final section of the course brought the groups together again to share the information collected. A more detailed view of some aspects of the criminal justice system was provided than was dealt with in the first part of the course or experienced during the second section. It was felt that a common input to clarify policy was needed. A prison governor, a judge, a probation officer with considerable experience of working with drug addicts, a research officer in the probation service, a university lecturer on social work, and a staff development officer were invited to offer seminars on the prison system, sentencing, drug abuse, research and training.

The English part of the exchange ended with a reception at the Martini Rooms, New Zealand House, when many of those who had been associated with the exchange courses were invited to meet the Polish visitors. Situated high in the centre of London the Martini Rooms provide a magnificent view over London and offer a particularly attractive setting for such an occasion. More informal gatherings were arranged during the third and final part of the exchange when the group were all staying in London. This was arranged so that the Polish visitors would have an opportunity to visit the main London sights, such as the Houses of Parliament, as well as going to the theatre and cinema, and doing some important shopping.

The ending of this programme was not final - the English group would be visiting Poland in the following year, and now that the partners knew each other the prospect of visiting Poland became even more real, and the English were keen to prepare themselves for the experience.

The first exchange with Poland in 1979 had been a very particular experience and the English group were concerned that they would be able to influence the way the programme was planned for their visit. They were particularly concerned that they would be able to visit probation offices and talk with probation officers about their work. The present composition of the exchange made for interesting discussions, but some of the English group felt they would benefit from discussion with practising probation officers. Before the Polish group left there was considerable discussion about the programme and one of the requests by the English group was that, if at all possible, the English group should be split into smaller groups of perhaps two pairs. It was recognised that in most cases it might be difficult for the Polish partner to accommodate the English partner, because of the shortage of housing and so it seemed likely that some might have to stay in hotels or hostels. Another request was that there should be a similar break down of time, with some days for information sharing at the beginning, followed by visits to work and home places, with a final few days to bring together the experience of the visits, both in England and in Poland. In the event both requests were granted, and while we were taken on some group visits in the first week, the time spent out in the country was in smaller groups and it was only necessary for five English people to stay in hostels, three of whom were staff members.

The visit to Poland took place in June 1985 and for various reasons required the group to move around the country a good deal. This provided the group with a valuable perception of different parts of Poland.

We arrived in Warsaw on 9 June and stayed in a hotel in the centre of the town for three nights. The first day consisted of visits to a correctional house for teenage girls, where the director was one of the exchange course members. We were provided with a valuable view of the positive side of institutional care and a first hand account by the director of his objectives.

We also visited a new initiative in the treatment of drug addicts, which followed a similar model to the Phoenix House, London, and the Synanon in the United States of America. The Monar centre has now been running for about four years, and represents a considerable breakthrough in the treatment of drug addicts in Poland. We met the director who has pioneered this centre and is developing other centres around the country, with the aim of creating a long term after care facility for those who have been through the system, come off drugs, and who are likely to need considerable help to continue with their abstinence. The drug problem in Poland is considerable, and is not helped by the poppy market which has always been part of the peasants' economy, initially in providing for the medical market and now, of course, is very much part of the underground drug scene. Legislation to prevent the growing of poppies is not seen as politically wise making the battle to restrict the amount of heroin available much more difficult.

The second day was spent at the Ministry of Justice, with inputs on the organisation and structure of the courts in Poland, the role and tasks of probation officers, and the structure of the Family Courts.

The following day we were taken by bus to Kazimierze, an ancient city about 100 miles from Warsaw where we spent the rest of the week discussing aspects of the Polish system.

We stayed in the conference centre of the Ministry of Justice, set in beautiful surroundings beside the River Vistula. At this point members of the exchange presented papers on aspects of their work in Poland and we were able to discuss in detail the work of the probation service, the legal system, provision of facilities for young people and explore the Family Diagnostic Centres, whose assessments are used extensively in courts when recommending sentences.

We returned to Warsaw on Friday afternoon and those of the party who were travelling to Krakow, or further north left that evening. The weekend was spent relaxing and sightseeing. The main work began on Monday morning when each group of Polish and English were engaged in their own programmes of visits to different institutions, courts and probation offices. The programme was closed in Warsaw when we all reassembled. There were several meetings, one at the Institute of Resocialisation at the University of Warsaw and another at the Ministry of Justice which was addressed by the Minister.

Bibliography

Ascherson, N., *The Polish August*, Viking, New York, 1982

Ash, Timothy Garton, *The Polish Revolution*, Coronet, London, 1985

Association of Municipal Corporations and County Council Associations, *The Seebohm Report - Study Conference*, London, 1968

Association of Directors of Social Services, *Children Still In Trouble*, London, 1985

Barker, Colin and Weber, Karen, *Solidarnosc: from Gdansk to Military Repression*, Socialist Workers' Party, London, 1982

Berlins, Marcel and Wansell, Geoffrey, *Caught in the Act: Children, Society and the Law*, Penguin, London, 1974

Bielen, Stefan, *Prevention and Combat of Children's and Juvenile Delinquency*. Paper prepared for Anglo-Polish Programme, 1985

Bridges, A., 'The Youth Custody Explosion', *Probation Journal*, June, 1985

British Broadcasting Corporation, *Panorma*, 9 December 1985

Browinski, J. and Jaworska, D.S., *Family Centres for*

Counselling and Diagnostics as Auxiliary Organs of Family Magistrates. Paper prepared for Anglo-Polish Exchange Programme, 1985

Bryant, M., Covington, C. and Himmel, S., *Fair Play: A Balanced Approach to Juvenile Justice*, 1981

Cavanagh, W.E., *Juvenile Courts, the Child and the Law*, Penguin, London, 1962

Celnik, D. et al, 'Management and Structure of the Polish Probation Services: Allocation of Resources', in Harper, John et al (eds.), *Assist and Befriend or Direct and Control*, North East London Polytechnic, 1982

Children and Young Persons' Act 1933, HMSO, 1933

Children and Young Persons' Act 1963, HMSO, 1963

Children and Young Persons' Act, 1969, HMSO, 1969

Children and Young Persons' Act (Scotland) 1937, HMSO, 1937

Children and Young Persons' Act (Scotland) 1968, HMSO, 1968

Children's Act 1908, HMSO, 1908

Children's Act 1948, HMSO, 1948

Cohen, S., *Visions of Social Control: Crime, Punishment and Classification*, Polity Press, Oxford, 1985

Cohen, S., 'The Punitive Century: Notes on the Dispersal of Social Control', *Contemporary Crises*, 1979

Committee of Inquiry into the United Kingdom Prison Services, *Report of the Committee*, HMSO, October 1979 (Cmnd 7673)

Committee on One Parent Families, *Report of the Committee (Finer Report)*, HMSO, 1974

Criminal Justice Act 1948, HMSO, 1948

Criminal Justice Act 1982, HMSO, 1982

Davies, Nick, *The Observer*, 8 December 1985

Dicey, A., *Lectures on the Relationship between Law and Public Opinion in England during the Nineteenth Century*, MacMillan, London, 1962

Dodwell, T. et al, 'Family Courts and Probation Centres in Poland', in Harper, John, et al (eds.), *Assist and Befriend or Direct and Control*, North East London Polytechnic, 1982

Downes, David and Rock, Paul, *Understanding Deviance*, Clarendon Press, Oxford, 1982

Emmins, Christopher, *Guide to Criminal Justice Act 1982*

Farringdon, D.P., 'Delinquency Prevention in the 1980s', *Journal of Adolescence*, 8, 1985

Fitzgerald, M. and Sim, J., *British Prisons*, Blackwell, Oxford, 1979

Fitzmaurice, C. and Pease, K., 'Prison Sentences and Population: a Comparison of Some European Countries', *Justice of the Peace*, 18 October 1982

Gibson, B., 'Custody and Young Offenders', *Justice of the Peace*, Vol. 149, No. 43, 26 October 1985

Goodman, Geoffrey, Pollution, *Social Interest and the Law?* Robertson, London, 1974

Guardian, Leading Article, 7 December 1985

Halecki, O., *A History of Poland*, Routledge, London, 1978

Hall, S., *Policing the Crisis: Mugging, the State and Law and Order*, MacMillan, London, 1978

Harper, John et al (eds.), *Assist and Befriend or Direct and Control*, North East London Polytechnic, 1982

Home Office, *The Child, the Family and the Young Offender*, HMSO, 1965 (Cmnd 2742)

Home Office, *Children in Trouble*, HMSO, 1968 (Cmnd 3601)

Home Office, *Criminal Careers of those born in 1953, 1958, 1963*, HMSO, Bulletin No.7, 1985

Home Office, *Criminal Statistics*, HMSO, 1985

Home Office, *Report of the Committee on Children and Young Persons (Ingleby Report)*, HMSO, 1960 (Cmnd 1191)

Home Office, *Statistical Bulletin*, HMSO, February 1985

Hough, M. and Moxon, D., 'Dealing with Offenders: Popular Opinions and Views of Victims', *Howard Journal*, Vol.24, No.3, August 1985

Johnson, G. et al, *Delinquency Prevention*, Office of Juvenile Justice and Delinquency Prevention, Washington, DC, 1981

Jones, M., *Crime, Punishment and the Press*, National Association for the Care and Resettlement of Offenders, London, 1980

Justice of the Peace, Family Courts, 22 January 1983

Kent Joint Social Services/Probation Research Group, *Statistics, November 1984 - April 1985*, Kent Social Services Department, Maidstone, 1985

King, R. and Morgan, R., *The Future of the Prison System*, Gower, Farnborough, 1980

Kolankiewicz, George, Review of 'Society and Deviance in Communist Poland: Attitudes towards Social Control' by Jerzy Kwasniewski, *British Journal of Criminology*, October 1985

Kudynski, Jerzy, *The Polish Legal System.* Paper prepared for Anglo-Polish Exchange Programme, 1985

Kudynski, Jerzy, *The System of Minors' Guardians in Poland (Probation Service for Juveniles).* Paper prepared for Anglo-Polish Exchange Programme, 1985

Lammich, S., 'The Polish Penal System', *Zeitschrift für Strafvollzug und Straffälligenhilfe*, Vol. 30, No.2, 1981 (in German)

Lang, K., *Military Institutions and the Sociology of War?* Sage, London, 1972

Lloyd, V. and Wagner, G., *The Camera and Dr. Barnardo*, Hertford, 1974

Majer, Janina, *Probation towards Adults.* Paper prepared for Anglo-Polish Exchange Programme, 1985

Manchester, A.H., 'Impression of the Scottish System of Juvenile Justice', *Justice of the Peace*, Vol. 149, No. 35, 31 August 1985

Mason, David S., *Public Opinion and Political Change in Poland 1980 - 1982*, Cambridge University Press, 1985

Milham, S., *Address to All Party Parliamentary Group for Children*, House of Lords, 6 May 1981

Miller, Jerome, *Decarceration*, Address to Southampton University, 7 November 1985

Moczydlowski, P., 'Types of Penal Institution, Economic Organisation and Inmate Social Structure: Some Polish Examples', *International Journal of the Sociology of Law*, Vol. II, 1983

Morgan, Patricia, *Delinquent Fantasies*, Temple Smith, London, 1975

Morris, A., et al, *Justice for Children*, MacMillan, London, 1981

Mosciskier, Andrzej, *Criminality in Poland.* Paper prepared for Anglo-Polish Exchange Programme, 1985

Murch, M., *Justice and Welfare in Divorce*, Sweet and Maxwell, 1980

National Association for the Care and Resettlement of Offenders, *Juvenile Crime: Briefing Paper*, NACRO, London, May 1985

Nocon, A., 'Social Welfare Provision in Poland', *Social Policy and Administration*, Vol.16, No.3, Autumn 1982

Parsloe, P., *Juvenile Justice in Britain and the United States*, Routledge, London, 1978

Pease, K., 'What Risk of Reconviction of Juveniles?', *Justice of the Peace*, 25 May 1985

Penal Code of the Polish People's Republic (American Series for Penal Codes), Sweet and Maxwell, 1973

Piechowiak, Z., *Post-penitentiary Aid and After-Care in Poland.* Paper prepared for Anglo-Polish Exchange Programme, 1985

Poland, *Official Handbook, Acts of 26th October 1982*, English translation prepared for Anglo-Polish Exchange Programme, 1985

Poland, *Social Statistics, 1984*, English translation prepared for Anglo-Polish Exchange Programme, 1985

Poland in Brief, Polish Interpress Agency, Warsaw, 1980

Pratt, J., 'Delinquency as a Scarce Resource', *Howard Journal*, Vol.24, No.2, May 1985

Pytka, L., *Some Principles of Resocialisation Education and Correctional Treatment in Poland.* Paper prepared for Anglo-Polish Exchange Programme, 1985

Raynor, P., *Social Work, Justice and the Community: Some Problems of Goals and Values*, National Association of Probation Officers Professional Conference, Centurion Press, 1985

Reiner, Robert, *The Politics of the Police*, Wheatsheaf, Brighton, 1985

Rodgers, B. et al, *A Study of Social Policy: A Comparative Approach*, Allen and Unwin, London, 1975

Rogala, J., *Drug Addiction in Poland.* Paper prepared for Anglo-Polish Exchange Programme, 1985

Rogala, J., *The Rules of Therapy of the Young Drug Addicts in the Rehabilitation Centre 'Monar'.* Paper prepared for Anglo-Polish Exchange Programme, 1985

Ruane, K., *The Polish Challenge*, BBC Publications, London, 1982

Rutherford, A., *Prisons and the Process of Justice: The Reductionist Challenge*, Heinemann, London, 1984

Rutter, M., and Giller, H., *Juvenile Delinquency: Trends and Perspectives*, Penguin, London, 1983

Ryan, Mick, *The Politics of Penal Reform*, Longman, London 1983

Rzeplinski, A., 'Prison Staff in Poland in the Light of Legal Regulations and Actual Practice', *International Journal of Offender Therapy and Comparative Criminology*, Vol.27, No.2, 1983

Rzeplinski, A., 'Prisoners' Rights in Poland', *International Journal of Offender Therapy and Comparative Criminology*, Vol.25, No.2, 1981

Samuels, A., 'Community Service: How Many Hours, How Long?'

Justice of the Peace, Vol. 149, No. 39, 28 September 1985

Scarman, Baron, *The Brixton Disorders 10th - 12th April, 1981*, HMSO, 1982

Schopflin, George, 'How the General Stays on Top', *The Times*, 7 November 1985

Scottish Home and Health Department, Committee on Children and Young Persons, *Children and Young Persons Scotland (Kilbrandon Report)*, HMSO, 1964

Steven, Stewart, *The Poles*, MacMillan, London, 1982

Stojanowska, Wanda, *The Family Courts in Poland*. Paper prepared for Anglo-Polish Exchange Programme, 1985

Sunday Times, *MORI Opinion Poll*, 3 November 1985

Szczepanski, J., *Polish Society*, Random House, New York, 1970

Taylor, Ian, *Law and Order: Arguments for Socialism*, MacMillan, London, 1981

Taylor, Stan, 'Theoretical Approaches to the Explanation of the Riots', in Bunyan, John, (ed), *Scarman and After*, Pergamon, Oxford, 1983

Tebbit, Norman, Disraeli Lecture, *The Guardian*, 15 November 1985

Thomas, J.E., *The English Prison Officer Since 1850*, Routledge, London 1972

Thomas, J.E., 'The Influence of the Prison Service', in Walker, N., (ed.), *Penal Policy Making in England*, Cambridge, 1977

Thomas, J.E., and Pooley, R., *The Exploding Prison*, Junction Books, London, 1980

Townsend, P., '14 Million Poor', *Community Care*, 25 October, 1979

Tutt, N, 'Justice or Welfare?', *Social Work Today*, Vol.14, No.7, October 1982

Tutt, N., *Violence*, HMSO, 1976

Walker, Hilary, and Beaumont, Bill, (eds.) *Working with Offenders*, MacMillan Education, London, 1985

Walker, N., 'Do Sentences Affect Public Disapproval?', *British Journal of Criminology*, 1982

Walker, N., 'The Misuse of Probation', *Probation*, March 1966

Williams, J.E. Hall, *The English Penal System in Transition*, Butterworth, London, 1970

Witts, A., *Something Broken in Poland*, Radio Documentary, October, 1985

Wojciechowski, S, 'Poland's New Priority: Human Welfare' in Thursz, D., and Vigilante, J.L., *Meeting Human Needs: An Overview of Nine Countries*, Sage, London 1975

Ziemska, Maria, *Divorce in Poland and the Adaptation of the Broken Family to the Post-Divorce Situation.* Paper prepared for Anglo-Polish Exchange Programme, 1985

Ziemska, Maria, *Early Child Care in Poland*, Gordon and Breach, New York, 1978